CHRISTIAN
DIVORCE
CHRISTIAN
REMARRIAGE

By Robert Eldredge Sr.

CHOICE
PUBLICATIONS

Unless otherwise indicated, all Scripture quotations are from the King James Version of the Bible

Scripture taken from the Holy Bible, NIV. Copyright 1973,1978, 1984 by New York International Bible Society. Used by permission of Zondervan Corporation. All rights reserved.

Cover design by Joseph Eldredge

Set in arial font

ISBN 979-8-9882132-3-9

C O N T E N T S

FORWARD

Much injustice has been done to the body of Christ because of religious prejudice and the improper interpretation of Scriptures. As a result, many divorced or remarried Christians have suffered needlessly from discrimination, loneliness, guilt, and shame.

I recently heard of a pastor who resigned from his church just because he and his wife had divorced. Even though the cause of the divorce was his former wife's adultery, the pastor said he still had to resign because 'he did not want to bring reproach to the ministry'.

What reproach?

If there was any reproach, it should have been upon the wife who committed the adultery, and certainly not upon the innocent and faithful husband!

And what a waste!

The pastor had obviously spent many years in study and prayer, and his ministry experience could have been useful to the body of Christ! Why should he be forced to get a secular job just because of something his ex-wife had done?

Another person that I knew personally also suffered much injustice as well. Even though her former husband had remarried, she was told at her Bible college that she could never marry as long as he was still alive! At first, she believe this lie because she still had suppressed feelings of guilt her failed marriage.

Later, she met and fell in love with a Christian man who had never been married before. She began to question what she had been taught and decided to do her own Bible study. Since her former husband had remarried, she believed she should be free to remarry. However, when she revealed her intentions, their pastor refused to perform the ceremony.

Eventually, they did find a pastor who was willing to "take a chance" and let them have a church wedding. Afterwards, they joined a different church, but the unjust discrimination still continued. Just because one of them had been divorced and remarried, they were now BOTH forever banned from holding any offices in the church!

Many other Christians have also suffered needlessly just because they were once divorced. Sometimes gossip is spread around the church that divorced people are either sexually promiscuous or "much greater sinners" and should therefore be avoided!

Those who have remarried are persecuted even more! In the Roman Catholic church, they are refused holy communion! In Protestant churches they are often refused positions of leadership as pastors, teachers, or deacons! Some are even refused permission to sing in the choir, and in a few extreme cases, they are even denied church membership!

In short, it is not uncommon for divorced Christians to be treated by their fellow Christians as second-class citizens in the Kingdom of God! I have therefore tried to answer every possible question a person might ask about marriage, divorce, and remarriage. It is my intention to make the interpretation of Scripture so crystal clear that the reader will never be bound by the legalistic and judgmental "traditions of men"!

1

The Traditions of Men

Roman Catholic and Protestant ministers or priests are very strongly influenced by their church traditions. They are even threatened with possible transfer or dismissal if they do not adhere to the traditional doctrines of their church.

About two thousand years ago, the apostle Paul warned us of the danger in following church leaders who base their theology upon the "traditions of men" and worldly principles, rather than the divine revelations and teachings of our Lord Jesus Christ.

Colossians 2:8 "Beware lest any man spoil you through philosophy and vain deceit, after the traditions of men, after the rudiments [principles] of the world, and not after Christ. "

No church is perfect, so this warning still applies today!

Every church has some doctrines that came from the traditions and opinions of men, rather than from God. As a matter of fact, that is why we have so many denominations! Every new church was originally formed because their founders' believed doctrines that were different from the other churches. That is why they were founded.

Well, they cannot all be right!

There is nothing wrong with being an active member of a denomination, but those who follow without question all of the traditional views of their particular church will eventually become deceived if they do not do their own Bible study and seek understanding from God.

The Pharisees were a separate denomination (of Judaism) when Jesus walked this earth. Although their tradition of washing their hands before eating was a good one, they had made it into a sacred religious act.

When they saw that the disciples of Jesus did not always wash their hands, they asked him, "Why do thy disciples transgress the traditions of the elders?" Jesus replied, "Why do ye also transgress the commandment of God by your tradition?"

He then rebuked them for their practice of dedicating elderly parents to God just to avoiding taking care of them, "Thus have ye made the commandment of God of none effect by your tradition. Ye hypocrites, well hath Isaiah prophesied of you saying,

"This people draw nigh unto me with their lips, but their heart is far from me. But in vain do they worship me, teaching for doctrines the commandments of men!" (Matthew 15:1-9)

Later Jesus was even more bold when he told them face to face that they were all 'blind guides, who strain out the gift and swallow a camel!' (Matthew 23:24) In other words, they nitpicked over very trivial issues and commandments while completely ignoring the much more important issues.

Many church leaders still do that today.

My mother was a pious Roman Catholic for her entire life. She made sure that all of her children were baptized and confirmed. When my older brother, Clyde, decided to marry a Protestant woman, this created a serious religious problem.

Roman Catholic traditions at that time did not permit marriage outside of the church. The local parish priest told my mother that she should not attend her son's Protestant wedding because that would be showing approval of the so called "sin" of marrying outside of the Roman Catholic church...

My mother was a widow at the time, so she asked me what I thought. Even though I was only a young teenager, I remember telling her that I believed the church was only a guide and that she should follow her own heart. She agreed and decided to go to her son's wedding in spite of the "traditions of men"!

The more important issue in this case was obviously not the traditional views of her church, but rather that she should be allowed to express her love and support for her son and for his future bride.

I still believe in following your heart, for God often speaks through your "conscience", but now I add the condition that the desires of your heart must also be in complete agreement with the written Word of God, the Holy Bible.

2 Timothy 3:16 "All Scripture is given by inspiration of God, and is profitable for doctrine, for reproof, for correction, for instruction in righteousness, that the man of God may be perfect, thoroughly furnished unto all good works."

HOW TO INTERPRET SCRIPTURE

In order to 'rightly divide the word of truth' and separate it from the traditions and doctrines of men, you will have to know a little bit about how to properly interpret Scripture.

- Scripture must always be interpreted in context, so you should study the meaning of the preceding and the following verses as well.
- You should not try to establish or confirm a doctrine without the support of at least one other Scripture.
- Your interpretation must always agree with original intent (called "exegesis") of the Scriptures.

Most Bible scholars agree on these three basic principles, but they use different methods in developing their complex and varied doctrines on divorce and remarriage.

The first method that many theologians use is what I call the "legalistic" approach. This is the use of the rules and principles of Scripture as inflexible law. This is the most common approach, and much better of the two, but often breaks down into "legalism" by adherence to the "letter law" rather than to the "spirit of the law".

The second method is what I call the "idealized approach. Since the continuation of a marriage is the ideal, those who use this approach claim that there is never any justification for a divorce.

It is from this approach that you get radical views, such as the breaking-up of a marriage because the couple are said to be continuously committing adultery!

My own theological approach, if any, may best be described as one of the heart, combined with my belief in a loving God and the inspiration and infallibility of the holy Scriptures. I feel compassion for divorced people, who are caught in the middle of this theological debate, and I believe the truth of God's word is able to set them free.

I believe God also feels the same way, so I expect that all of my conclusions will be in full agreement with the Bible. As a matter of fact, if you do not continuously see God as a loving and compassionate Father, then you will miss the true intent of the Scriptures and be just as much bound by legalism and self-righteousness, just as are some church theologians.

Even as I write this, I am aware that I am "stepping on the toes" of many theologians, who have spent hours of research and study. Nevertheless, I am determined to present this subject as clearly as I can, so that any lay person can understand it. He is the one, and not the theologian, whose life is drastically affected by the interpretation of Scripture.

This reminds me of a story:

A circus star was about to cross the Niagara Falls on a tightrope while pushing a wheelbarrow. He asked the theologian, "Do you believe I can do it?" The theologian answered boldly, "Of course you can do it!" The circus star then replied, "Since you believe I can do it, I want you to ride in the wheelbarrow!"

While the questions of divorce and remarriage are theoretical issues to the theologian, they are extremely important life changing issues to the divorced or remarried person! I have therefore addressed this book primarily to the lay person who has been divorced, and not to the theologian.

DISAGREEMENTS

Lay people often assume that priests and ministers must know the answers to at least the basic questions concerning divorce and remarriage because most of them have been to a seminary or a Bible school. Yes, they are taught what answers to give you, but even the theologians in their own church do not agree among themselves on many of these issues.

Someone once said jokingly that if you could lay all of the theologians in the world on the ground end to end, they still would not be able to reach a conclusion!

And their complex and varied theories have now become so confusing and complex, that most lay people and local pastors just "give up" and accept the traditional views of their own particular denomination.

In 1937, the influence of the Roman Catholic traditions caused the Republic of Ireland to institute a constitutional ban on all divorce. This was strictly enforced for almost six decades before it was finally repealed in 1995. Even then, the influence of the Roman Catholic church was so strong that it just barely passed with a vote of 50.2% to 49.8%.

Protestant churches are not exempt from theological disagreements. A major Protestant denomination has been debating for decades whether or not to allow the ordination of divorced and remarried ministers. They recently voted against allowing their ordination by a vote of 60% to 40%. The majority voted the wrong way, but I want the reader to know that these and similar issues are still debated today.

The Roman Catholic church is well known for its position that ultimate authority begins with the Pope and passes on down through the hierarchal structure. The local priest that you may have asked for advice would be at the very bottom of this hierarchy, so he has absolutely no authority at all to change any church doctrines.

Therefore, even if your local priest should have different views, it is not likely that he would tell you. If a priest disobeys the rules of his church, he could be transferred to a remote parish, defrocked as a priest, or, in extreme cases, he could even be excommunicated from the church.

Martin Luther was an Augustinian monk who was later ordained as a priest on April 4, 1507. He never intended to start a new church or denomination. He only wanted to correct what he sincerely believed were erroneous traditions and doctrines in his church.

Among many other things, Luther objected to the traditional view that a person must always remain single after a divorce. Even though he had a doctorate degree from the University of Wittenberg, he was eventually excommunicated in 1521 when he continued to object to church traditions.

The threat of being excommunicated or transferred still exists today. One Roman Catholic priest personally confided to me about his concern that something like that might happen to him. He said to me,

"What would I do? This is all I know! I don't have any job skills! How would I be able to make a living?"

If you belong to an Eastern or a Protestant church, don't think you have escaped from the influence of church traditions. The Eastern churches are almost as old as the Roman Catholic church. And Protestant churches have not only passed down the traditions of their founders, but they have had almost five centuries to develop new ones.

The pastors of Eastern and Protestant churches are also threatened with the loss of ministerial credentials, and maybe even their churches, if they do not obey their church traditions. The loss of ministerial credentials, and possibly their church, are very serious threats to pastors. Even if they do not fully agree with their church traditions, most pastors will think twice before risking so much for a church member.

And even if a pastor should happen to be in full agreement with all of the traditions and doctrines of his church, he may not know very much about the issues of divorce and remarriage.

It is just not possible for a local pastor to know, and to be theologically correct, on every single issue.

I am not suggesting that should never seek advice or counsel from your church pastor. Seeking counsel is normally very wise. But if you do not pray and do your own study, you will never know how to "rightly divide the word of truth".

2 Timothy 2:15 "Study to show thyself approved unto God, a workman that needeth not to be ashamed, rightly dividing the word of truth. "

Let us now begin our study of divorce and remarriage by first determining exactly what the Bible *really does say* about what constitutes a valid marriage.

2

Marriage is for Life

Marriage is an exclusive and intimate union of a man and a woman that is established when they make a covenant to leave their parents and form a new family unit. It is a pure and holy union that is similar to the eternal union of Jesus Christ and his Church.

Several years ago, I read about a "commune" of young people who wanted to get away from all of the restraints of society. They were looking for freedom from every personal commitment, including the lifetime marriage commitment.

The reporter lived with them for a while and observed that, in spite of their lack of a formal commitment, a couple would eventually pair off and restrict their sexual relations to each other. If anyone tried to become involved with "his girl" or "her man", extreme jealousy would rise up. The reporter said that it was just as if they were legally married.

The people in the commune were actually confirming the fact that, from the very beginning, God created men and women with an innate desire to join together in an exclusive union.

Jesus confirmed this later when he limited marriage to the union of only one man and one woman (Mark 10:8).

THE MARRIAGE COVENANT

The key to understanding divorce and remarriage is to recognize that marriage is established and maintained by a covenant.

A marriage begins when a man and a woman voluntarily make a covenant to leave their parents and cleave together as husband and wife for the rest of their lives.

In order to strengthen this lifetime commitment, the State of Louisiana became the first State in the Union to pass a law which took effect in 1997 called the "Covenant Marriage Act". Under this new law, couples are given the option to voluntarily agree to premarital and pre-divorce counseling and to give up their legal rights to a "no-fault" divorce. Then, unless it can be proven in court that there has been adultery, abuse, or abandonment, etc., the law requires a minimum two-year waiting period before the couple can ever be granted a legal divorce.

This law draws attention to the fact that marriage is established by a covenant. In Malachi 2:14, God referred to a married woman as "the wife of thy covenant". In Ezekiel 16:8, God referred to his own spiritual marriage covenant with Israel when He said, "Yea, I swore unto thee, and entered into a covenant with thee, and thou becamest mine."

Once a marriage covenant has been made, the man and the woman become "one" in the sight of both God and man. Just as two people become "one" by their covenant in a business partnership, so do a man and a woman become "one" by their covenant in a marriage partnership.

Genesis 2:23-24 "And Adam said, this is now bone of my bones, flesh of my flesh; she shall be called woman, because she was taken out of man. Therefore shall a man leave his father and mother and shall cleave to his wife; and they shall be one flesh."

The word "cleave" means to permanently join together, so marriage was intended to be a lifetime commitment. A temporary agreement with a prostitute or someone else will also make a man and a woman "one flesh", but this type of union is strictly forbidden. (See 1 Corinthians 6:13-20)

And since marriage is supposed to be a lifetime commitment for the rest of your life, annulments are unbiblical. Once marriage covenants are confirmed by the exchange of vows, they cannot be "annulled" by man.

Galatians 3:15 "Though it be but a man's covenant, yet if it be confirmed, no man disannulled or addeth to it."

It is actually the couple's own vows that confirm their lifetime marriage commitment. A priest, minister, or rabbi only witnesses and legally records the event. Marriage vows made before a Justice of the Peace are therefore just as binding in the sight of God.

A typical marriage ceremony normally includes a promise to stay united together for the rest of their earthly lives "whether in sickness or in health, for richer or poorer, for better or for worse, until death do us part." God always keeps his vows, and he expects us to do the same.

Numbers 30:2 "If a man vow a vow unto the Lord or swear an oath to bind his soul with a bond, he shall not break his word; he shall do according to all that proceedeth out of his mouth."

From the very beginning (and even unto this day) a Jewish marriage has always had two stages. The first one is called the "kiddushin" and the second one is called the "huppah".

The kiddushin is where the betrothal covenant is made. In ancient times, the betrothal covenant was confirmed either by a written or oral contract, by the exchange of money, or by the couple having sexual relations inside a private chamber. The latter method was abandoned around 500 BC, but it shows that a couple was already considered to be united as "one flesh" after they had made their betrothal covenant.

The 'huppah' is a public wedding ceremony, and it was originally a very festive celebration that would last for seven days. It would normally end with the bride and the groom leaving to have sexual relations inside a private bridal chamber at the home of the groom. (Judges 15:1)

The kiddushin and the huppah could be combined, but they were usually separated by a defined period of time. If a betrothed woman had sexual relations with any other man during this time, then both the man and the woman would be called adulterers and publicly stoned to death.

The fact that they were called adulterers, and that the punishment was the same as for adultery, is further proof that a marriage is established by a covenant alone, and that sexual intercourse is not really necessary in order to "complete "or "consummate" the marriage union.

WHAT GOD HAS JOINED TOGETHER...

When Jesus was asked if a man could divorce his wife for any reason whatsoever, he repeated what Adam had said about a man and a woman becoming united as "one flesh", and then he added, "What, therefore, God hath joined together, let not man put asunder." (Matthew 19:6)

This means that God ordained marriage to be an inseparable union for life, and no human being has the right to separate what God has joined together. However, this does not mean that married couples who were once joined together as "one flesh" can never be separated. It only means that they *should never* be separated!

We often do what we shouldn't do. It is called sin.

And the sin that separates what God had joined together is not the divorce itself, but the breaking of the marriage covenant that had once united them.

Various fourth century writers have taught that the words, "let not man put asunder" meant that marriage was "indissoluble". But marriage cannot be considered indissoluble because Moses and Jesus both allowed the dissolution of a marriage whenever a couple's marriage vows were broken by sexual immorality.

Some other theologians have thought the words, "God hath joined together", were a reference to sexual intercourse. This led to the development of the traditional doctrine that a marriage is not fully completed or "consummated" until after the couple have had sexual intercourse.

But how can someone be only half married?

Can a woman be only half pregnant?

And if sexual intercourse were necessary to complete a marriage union, why was a written divorce required to end a betrothal relationship? And why were those who were unfaithful during their betrothal period called adulterers and then stoned to death?

Anyway, this erroneous doctrine is easily refuted by the Lord's next words, "let not man put asunder". Since the couple are never to be separated, this cannot possibly be a reference to sexual intercourse.

Sometimes Christians will think that the words, "God hath joined together" must mean that God has specifically chosen their marriage partners. This is not necessarily true. God has a perfect plan for your life, and He will help you find a compatible mate if you pray for this, but He will never take away your free will to choose.

Marriage on earth is very similar to our spiritual marriage with Jesus. God will draw you towards his Son (John 6:44), but you still must choose whether or not you want to accept Him. As with earthly marriages, you must first enter into a marriage covenant with Jesus before He becomes your eternal bridegroom.

Revelation 19:9 "Blessed are they who are called unto the marriage supper of the lamb [Jesus]."

As Christians, we are all looking forward to that glorious day!

LET NO MAN SEPARATE...

During the first few centuries of Christianity, the church leaders recognized that marriage was a pure and holy union, but it was discouraged because of their severe persecution by the Roman government and the hope that Jesus would soon return.

When the apostle Paul wrote to the church in Corinth around 56 AD, he said,

"The time is short; it remaineth that both they that have wives be as though they had none."

(1 Corinthians 7:29)

This was understandable at the time because so many Christians were then being imprisoned, tortured, and even put to death. However, the persecution of Christians ended abruptly in 313 AD when the Roman Empire granted freedom for all religions by issuing the Edict of Milan.

Christianity was then publicly endorsed by the Roman emperor, Constantine, so it immediately became "politically correct" to profess Christianity! This eventually led to the corruption of the church leadership by people who joined only for political reasons. Illiteracy was common, so the newly formed government-approved church hierarchy was composed mostly of those from the wealthy and well-educated ruling class.

The Church leaders continued to discourage marriage, but now for completely different reasons.

Apparently, these newly appointed church leaders overreacted to the sexual immorality that was prevalent in the wealthy ruling class, and then went to the other extreme by promoting complete abstinence from all sexual relations, even in marriage!

These fourth century leaders also promoted asceticism (extreme self-denial) as a way of gaining God's approval. They encouraged total abstinence from all sexuality and demeaned the institution of marriage itself by saying that it was substantially inferior to a single celibate life. Ambrose and Jerome were probably the most influential writers who supported these extreme beliefs.

Ambrose was a Roman governor before he became Bishop of Milan in 374 AD. He felt guilty because of his privileged birth, so he "immediately distributed his share of the family wealth to the poor and set an example of strict asceticism in the episcopal household."[1]

---

[1] New Catholic Encyclopedia, Volume I, McGraw-Hill, New York, 1967, page 373

Although he was never married, he was the first Bishop to write at length about sexual issues in the church. As might be expected, he zealously promoted his own celibate lifestyle as the ideal for both married and unmarried Christians.

Because marriage permitted sexual intercourse, he felt that it was considerably inferior to a single celibate life. And since church leaders were supposed to be examples of purity and holiness, he believed that all clergy should be single and celibate.

He apparently ignored the fact that the apostle Peter was married and, according to Clement of Alexandria, he also had children! In addition, most of the early church leaders were married, and some of them even brought their wives along with them on their missionary journeys (see 1 Corinthians 9:5).

Jerome was also unmarried, and he went even further in discouraging marriage. He was convinced that sexual relations were intrinsically evil even within marriage, and therefore should be "tolerated" only for the purpose of conceiving children. He once said, "Marriage is only one degree less sinful than fornication." [2]

---

[2] A History of Christianity, by Paul Johnson, Macmillan Publishing Co, New York, 1967, pages 109-110

Since both Ambrose and Jerome were later canonized as "saints" by the Roman Catholic church, their beliefs on human sexuality have had a very strong influence upon succeeding generations. This has been especially true for those who were brought up in parochial schools.

While abstinence is important before marriage, these beliefs have made some married people unable to enjoy normal sexual relations without feeling guilty. If you also feel this way, this can be easily dispelled by asking yourself the following rhetorical questions:

- Since Adam and Eve had not yet sinned when they were told to "be fruitful and multiply", how were they supposed to obey God if sex was sinful?
- Since God never tempts anyone to sin, why would he tell Adam and Eve to "be fruitful and multiply" if sex was sinful?

In short, sexual relations are pure and holy as long as they are kept within the covenant of a monogamous marriage relationship. It is only the misuse of human sexuality outside of the lifetime marriage commitment that is wrong.

HUMAN SEXUALITY IS GOOD

Everything that God has made and ordained is good. When God made the earth, the sun, the moon, the stars, animals, birds, and sea life, "God saw that it was good." But he was even more pleased with his creation after he made Adam and Eve, because he then said, "It was very good." (Genesis 1:31).

Ecclesiastes 9:9: "Live joyfully with the wife whom thou lovest all the days of the life of thy vanity, which He [God] hath given thee under the sun."

The Song of Solomon even uses the enjoyment of sex within marriage as an allegory to our love relationship with God! Even when conception is not possible, there is nothing immoral about the mutual enjoyment of sexual relations. If God had intended sex to be only for procreation, he would have made us so that every sexual act would result in the conception of children.

1 Corinthians 7:3-4 "The husband should fulfill his marital duty to his wife, and likewise the wife to her husband. The wife's body does not belong to her alone but also to her husband. In the same way, the husband's body does not belong to him alone, but also to his wife. " (New International Version)

The perversion and exploitation of human sexuality by worldly people should not keep Christians from enjoying the meaningful sexual relationships that can only thrive within a loving and a Christ centered marriage relationship.

Hebrews 13:4 "Marriage is honorable in all, and the bed undefiled, but whoremongers and adulterers, God will judge."

GOD'S NATURE AND MARRIAGE'S PURPOSE

The "oneness" of God was revealed to us in the Jewish Shema, which begins with, "Hear O Israel, the Lord our God is one Lord" (Deuteronomy 6:4, Mark 12:29).

The "triune" nature of God as three "persons" was revealed to us when the Holy Spirit of God came upon Jesus, and God the Father acknowledged him as his "own beloved Son". (Matthew 3:16-17)

Since God made us in his own image, I do not find it at all surprising that our family unit is very similar to his own triune nature. Although equal in divine nature, and united in perfect harmony as one God, each person of the Godhead has a separate function and experience.

- The role of God the Father is similar to that of a husband who is the head of a human family unit. (1 Corinthians 11:3).
- The role of God the Holy Spirit is similar to that of a wife who builds and nurtures a human family unit. (John 14:16).
- The role of God the Son is similar to that of the first-born son of a human family unit (Colossians 1:15).

And when we meditate upon the beautiful love relationship that God already has within himself, and how harmoniously they function together in their different roles, then we can better understand his perfect plan for earthly husbands, wives, and their children.

It should be obvious that having children is the primary purpose of sex and marriage, since our physical bodies were specifically designed by God for this purpose.

However, many people marry for other reasons, and they really do not want to have any children. Then if children are un-intentionally conceived, they will sometimes desert, divorce, or have an abortion, in order to escape from the responsibility of raising children.

The primary purpose of marriage from God's point of view is to have and to raise godly children. He united couples as one flesh "that he might seek a godly seed. " (Malachi 2:15) From the very beginning, God exhorted Adam and Eve to have lots of children.

Genesis 1:28 "And God blessed them, and God said unto them, Be fruitful and multiply, and replenish the earth, and subdue it; and have dominion over the fish of the sea, and over the fowl of the air, and over every living thing that moves upon the earth."

Other godly men, like Noah (Genesis 9:1) and Jacob (Genesis 35:11), were also told to "be fruitful and multiply" And the Jews who were exiled to Babylon were also exhorted to "beget sons and daughters", so that their numbers would increase in the land. (Jeremiah 29:6)

God's ultimate plan was, and still is, to fill the earth with a godly race of people who will be redeemed from sin, and who will have intimate fellowship with him throughout eternity!

A secondary purpose of marriage is to prevent sexual immorality by satisfying a person's sexual desires. As the apostle Paul so frankly put it:

1 Corinthians 7:8-9 "Now to the unmarried and the widows I say: It is good for them to stay unmarried, as I am. But if they cannot control themselves, they

should marry, for it is better to marry than to burn with passion. " (New International Version)

In the ancient Jewish culture, parents prevented immorality by encouraging their children to marry while they were very young. Everyone was expected to marry, so marriages were often arranged before they reached puberty. The minimum age was later set at thirteen for boys and twelve for girls.

Marital relations will normally satisfy each other's sexual desires and help avoid temptation. That is why the apostle Paul advised husbands and wives not to refuse each other's sexual desires, except by mutual consent whenever praying or fasting.

1 Corinthians 7:2-5 "Nevertheless, to avoid fornication, let every man have his own wife, and let every woman have her own husband. Let the husband render unto the wife due benevolence, and likewise also, the wife unto her husband.

According to ancient Jewish laws (Exodus 21:10-11), the refusal of conjugal rights was a violation of the marriage covenant and sufficient cause for a divorce. In his early writings, Martin Luther also considered this as a possible cause for a divorce.

The first human being, whom we call Adam, was made in the image of God, so he was neither male nor female. He loved and worshiped his creator, and his natural human nature was perfect because he was made in the image of God.

Then God said, "It is not good that man should be alone" (Genesis 2:18) so he put Adam to sleep and made a second human being from a portion of his body. Eve was created female, and Adam's body was changed to become male.

Since Eve was "taken out of" Adam's body (Genesis 2:23), this left him no longer complete in expressing the full nature of God. And since Eve was created from only a portion of Adam, she was also incomplete in expressing the full nature of God. Thus,

- The natural human nature of a woman has some of the characteristics of God that the man does not have. Thus,
- The natural human nature of a man has some of the characteristics that the woman does not have.

Men and women are separate creations who not only need each other for procreation, but also to fully express the nature and character of God on earth. It is therefore morally pure and perfectly natural for a man to desire a wife; and for a woman to desire a husband.

Proverbs 18:22 "Whoso findeth a wife findeth a good thing and obtaineth favor from the Lord. "

SINGLES AND THE CHURCH

Even if you prefer to remain single and do not want to get married, you can still express the nature and character of God simply by yielding to the spirit of Christ in your heart.

Colossians 2:10 "For in him [Jesus] dwelleth all the fullness of the Godhead bodily. And ye are complete in him who is the head of all principality and power."

When you yield to your new spiritually reborn nature, then it does not matter whether you are a man or a woman, for the spirit of Christ is neither male nor female.

Galatians 3:27-28 "For as many of you as, have been baptized [immersed] into Christ, have put on Christ. There is neither Jew nor Greek, there is neither bond [slave] nor free, there is neither male nor female, for ye are all one in Christ Jesus.

And, according to the apostle Paul, it is even better to remain single and unmarried, if it is your heart's desire to serve the Lord more fully.

1 Corinthian 7:32-33 "He that is unmarried careth for the things that belong to the Lord, how he may please the Lord; but he that is married careth for the things that are of the world, how he may please his wife.

Jesus also acknowledged that some will not marry because:

1. They were born physically incapable of marriage, or
2. They were made physically incapable of marriage by men, or
3. They have, like the apostle Paul, voluntarily chosen to remain single in order to better serve the kingdom of God (Matthew 19:12)

Just as we become "one flesh "when we make an earthly marriage covenant with our spouse, so we become "one spirit" when we make a spiritual marriage covenant with our Lord and Savior, Jesus Christ.

1 Corinthians 6:16-17 "For two, saith he, shall be one flesh, but he that is joined to the Lord is one spirit."

Paul calls this, 'a great mystery.'

Ephesians 5:22-32 "Wives, submit yourselves unto your own husbands, as unto the Lord. For the husband is the head of the wife, even as Christ is the head of the church; and He is the savior of the body. Therefore, as the church is subject unto Christ, so let the wives be to their own husbands in everything.

Husbands, love your wives, even as Christ loved the church, and gave himself for it, that He might sanctify and cleanse it with the washing of water by the word; that He might present it to himself a glorious church, not having spot or wrinkle, or any such thing; but that it should be holy and without blemish.

So ought men to love their wives as their own bodies. He that loves his wife, loves himself. For no man ever hated his own, but nourisheth and cherisheth it, even as the Lord the church; for we are members of His body, of His flesh, and of His bones. For this cause, shall a man leave his father and mother, and shall be joined unto his wife, and they two shall be one flesh.

This is a great mystery, but I speak concerning Christ and the church."

ETERNITY AND TRIAL

Marriage as we now know it will not exist in eternity. Our ultimate destiny as Christians is to be formally united forever, not with each other, but with our Lord Jesus Christ at the "marriage supper of the Lamb". (Revelation 19:7)

When we die, we will be transformed both physically and spiritually, and sexual relationships and earthly marriage will be no longer.

Luke 20-34-36 "The children of this world marry and are given in marriage; but they who shall be accounted worthy to obtain that world, and the resurrection from the dead, neither marry, nor are given in marriage. Neither can they die anymore; for they are equal unto the angels, and they are the children of God, being children of the resurrection."

Because there will be no more death, there will no longer be any need for sexual reproduction. But this does not mean that there will be no distinction between male and female personalities. Jesus died to save our souls (our mind, will, and emotions) so the individual characteristics of each soul, purified from the stain of sin, will still be retained.

If you are concerned about the loss of sexual pleasure in eternity, remember that God has already prepared something for us that is even better.

1 Corinthians 2:9 "But as it is written [Isaiah 64:4], Eye hath not seen, nor ear heard, neither has it entered into the heart of man, the things which God hath prepared for them that love him."

Having been married for thirty years, I can certainly confirm that, as long as we live here on earth, we will always have conflicts to resolve and trials to overcome. When my wife and I were first married, I was looking forward to a long and happy relationship, and I really did not expect to have any unusual problems.

Our first major trial occurred less than two years after we were married. Without any warning, my wife had a sudden seizure and a colossal headache. We found out later that she had a "brain aneurysm", and she almost died when a blood vessel had burst inside her brain.

The doctors said she was very fortunate to have survived, but that the blood vessel was still leaking and if they did not operate, she would die. Even then, they said that she had only a fifty-fifty chance of surviving the brain operation.

God was still in control.

It "happened" that Dr. Neil Poppen wanted to demonstrate a new technique to visiting surgeons from several other countries and he needed a patient with exactly my wife's condition.

The other doctors told me at the time that he was considered to be the "best brain surgeon in the entire world." So not only did we have the best, but he also operated upon my wife free of charge!

Although the brain operation did save her life, she still had considerable brain damage from the initial attack. In addition, she had a partial paralysis and weakness on one side of her body. When she spoke or smiled, only one side of her mouth would move. Her memory loss was so bad that, in the beginning, she even forgot that we were married.

As you can imagine, the trauma caused her to have deep seated feelings of insecurity. Even up to a year or so later, she was very reluctant to go shopping alone. Since we had moved to a different location, she was afraid that she might forget how to get home.

Again, I believe God intervened.

Even though Dr. Poppen had said that the partial paralysis was permanent and would never go away, all of the symptoms gradually disappeared within about two years! Another doctor told me later that he considered her quick recovery from the partial paralysis and memory loss as "nothing less than miraculous"!

Because of the high risk that another weakened blood vessel might burst during childbirth, one doctor even refused to have her as a patient if we did not practice birth control. However, we prayed about this, and we both agreed to trust God and continue to have children.

Well, the rest is history!

We had five more children after the brain operation without any complications. Praise the Lord! In addition to raising our six children and the usual family duties, my wife served the Lord as a deaconess in our local church. She also remained active in prison ministry and in helping the poor until her death from cancer a few years ago.

What is the use of trials?

As in earthly marriages, some Christians will backslide and "divorce" Jesus whenever they encounter trials. But when trials are overcome or patiently endured, they produce fruit that is "much more precious than gold" (1 Peter 1:6-9).

Trials are opportunities to prove your love.

Although the Bible is filled with many promises of God for blessing and prospering his people while we are on this earth, our first commitment is to love and serve him regardless of our circumstances.

The apostle Paul suffered much injustice and persecution, and yet he concluded that there was nothing that could ever separate him from the love of God.

Romans 8:35-39 "What shall separate us from the love of Christ? Shall tribulation, or distress, or persecution, or famine, or nakedness, or peril, or sword? .... For I am persuaded that neither death, nor life, nor angels, nor powers, nor things present, nor things to come, nor height, nor depth, nor any other creature, shall be able to separate us from the love of God, which is in Christ Jesus our Lord."

If trials cannot separate us from the love of God, then neither should they separate a husband and a wife from the love that they have for each other.

And since the union of Adam and Eve could have lasted until the end of the age (Genesis 3:22), it is easy to see why it was never the perfect will of God to terminate any marriage with a divorce.

3

God Loves Divorced People

God loves divorced people, but He hates divorce! He allows divorce only because of the hardness of our hearts. Although the act of divorce itself is not a sin, it is caused by the sin of at least one of the partners.

God loves both you and your mate, so the only time He allows divorce is if a marriage covenant has already been broken. As was explained in the previous chapter.

The key to understanding divorce and remarriage is to recognize that marriage is established and maintained by a covenant.

Since the marriage union is established by a covenant, the breaking of that covenant will also break the marriage union. A written divorce is then allowed to confirm that the couple are no longer united by their covenant as one flesh.

Once you understand this very basic principle, it is relatively easy to determine whether or not divorce should be permitted. All you have to do is determine whether or not the person's marriage covenant has already been broken!

Divorce is not a sin.

That may have shocked you because most people automatically think of divorce as always being a sin And the Bible even says that God "hates" divorce, so why wouldn't it be a sin?

It is true that it would be a sin to file for a divorce if your spouse has been faithful and wants to stay with you. However, if your spouse has already broken your marriage covenant, then it would *not* be a sin to file for a divorce.

Divorce is always the result of sin, but the act of divorce itself is not necessarily a sin. It cannot always be wrong to divorce because a written divorce was allowed by God under the Law of Moses whenever there was sexual immorality.

This is important to know for the following reasons:

- If you have already been divorced, and think that divorce is always a sin, then you may be suffering needlessly from neurotic feelings of guilt.

- If you are still married to an unfaithful partner, and think that divorce is always a sin, then you may be suffering needlessly because you cannot consider divorce as an option.

But can it be *proven* that the act of divorce itself is not a sin? I am going to surprise you by saying "Yes"!

The absolute proof is that God did it!

God divorced Israel when it backslid and committed spiritual adultery by worshiping other gods. This has to be considered as adequate proof. Anything less would be accusing God of committing a sin.

I am sure that you wouldn't want to do that!

Jeremiah 3:8 "And I saw, when for all the causes whereby backsliding Israel committed adultery, I had put her away [divorced her and given her a bill of divorce "

Because of his special love for Abraham and his descendants, God had previously made their relationship analogous to a marriage when he said to Israel, "thy Maker is thine husband."

Isaiah 54:5 "For thy Maker is thine husband; the Lord of hosts is his name; and thy redeemer, the

Holy One of Israel; The God of the whole earth shall he be called."

But when they broke their covenant by worshiping other gods, he was then forced to terminate their relationship with a spiritual "divorce"! This not only confirms the fact that divorce is not a sin, but it also confirms the fact that there can be an "innocent party" who has done absolutely nothing at all to cause the divorce!

Although divorce is not a sin, it is still caused by the sin of at least one of the partners. In the above example, the unfaithfulness that caused the divorce was obviously done by Israel, and not by God! In the next chapter, you will find how the sin of sexual lust, which is a form of idolatry, can cause a spouse to become unfaithful; and why this is always considered as sufficient cause for a divorce.

Since you now know that God intended marriage to be the most beautiful human relationship we can have on earth, it really should not surprise you to find out that he "hates divorce"! However, many divorced people have become so conditioned by their own feelings of guilt and self-condemnation that they sometimes think this means that God also "hates" divorced people.

Nothing could be further from the truth! When God said he "hated" divorce, he was referring only to the divorce of a faithful wife. God has always allowed the divorce of an unfaithful wife, but he has never condoned the divorce of a faithful wife.

Malachi 2:14-16 " the Lord has been a witness between thee and the wife of thy youth, against whom thou hast dealt treacherously; yet she is thy companion, and the wife of thy covenant ... therefore take heed to your spirit, and let none deal treacherously against the wife of thy youth. For the Lord, the God of Israel, says that he hateth putting away [divorce], for one covereth violence with his garment, saith the Lord of hosts; therefore take heed to your spirit that ye deal not treacherously,"

In the preceding Scripture, the man who divorced his wife was said to have dealt "treacherously" with her because she had been faithful. If she were unfaithful, it wouldn't be called treachery! And God also hates it when a wife "treacherously" deserts her faithful husband.

Jeremiah 3:20 "Surely, as a wife treacherously departeth from her husband, so have ye dealt treacherously with me, O house of Israel, saith the Lord."

DIVORCE AND MOURNING

Yes, God does hate the "treachery" of divorcing a faithful spouse and the misery that it causes, but then again who doesn't hate divorce?

Who really wants to exchange love and companionship for emotional pain and loneliness?

Who really wants to exchange an intimate sexual relationship for a cold and unfriendly relationship?

Who really wants to be separated from their children, family, and longtime friends whom they still love?

Who really wants to have the financial burdens that almost always result from a divided household?

Everyone suffers at least some loss whenever there is a divorce. Even those who wanted the divorce will readily admit that it was extremely painful; and most of them would have preferred to save their marriages if they could.

The man usually complains that he has lost his wife, his house, his children, and now, to add insult to injury, he has to pay a large portion of his salary for the privilege.

The woman usually complains that she has lost her security, the support payments are not nearly enough, remarriage is very unlikely, and now she has all of the responsibility for raising the children.

The divorce process itself is also very cold cumbersome and intimidating. Now third parties are involved, who must be informed of intimate details that have been experienced over the years. There is just no way that this can be adequately done with biased testimony and a brief summary to a judge.

Former friends can become enemies when they testify in court for the other side. Lies, cover-ups, and gross exaggerations are common as they each try to defend their own positions. And when children are involved, bitter emotional custody suits can go on for years. Even after the custody issues are settled, the court ordered visiting rights are a very poor substitute for a loving relationship with both parents.

Visiting parents often have mixed emotions. They want to express their love for their children, but they still have suppressed anger towards their former spouses. Custody parents are sometimes rude and resentful because their own personal lives have been disrupted. And both parents usually resent the fact that they still have to deal with their ex-wives or ex- husbands.

In this chapter, you will find Biblical precepts on how you can become free from the negative emotions of grief, anger, depression, and unforgiveness. In later chapters, you will learn how you can overcome feelings of lust, guilt/ bitterness, and rejection.

Bear in mind that these Biblical precepts are limited to basic psychological principles, and they 'are not intended to replace individual counseling or medi-cal treatment whenever it should become necessary.

The stress of divorce has been rated by some psychologists as second only to the death of a spouse! I cannot tell you from personal experience about divorce, but I can tell you about how I felt shortly after the death of my own wife.

I missed the love and companionship the most.

I missed not having a marriage partner to share my feelings and experiences. I felt like part of me had been taken away because no one else knew the experiences that we had once shared. Children are a blessing, but they have their own lives to live, and they only partially fill the gap.

I also suffered from the lack of energy and purpose that many must feel after a divorce. My normal desires for achievement and enjoyment seemed to dissipate without a close companion to share it.

I often felt lonely and sad for no apparent reason. Nothing seemed to be funny, so I almost never laughed anymore. Sometimes it took an effort just to get out of bed in the morning.

These are just a few symptoms of grief. Many people have also experienced sleeplessness, inability to concentrate, forgetfulness, anxiety, or physical weakness.

If you have ever been divorced or widowed, then you may find it comforting to know that these symptoms are absolutely normal after such a great loss.

Whenever any emotion, whether it is positive or negative, becomes too much to contain, it is perfectly normal to release them with tears. Many saints of God have wept when the circumstances of their lives became overwhelming. When King David was under constant attack by his enemies he said, "I water my couch with my tears. Mine eye is consumed because of grief. " (Psalm 6:6-7)

Weeping is like an emotional safety valve. When the emotional pressure becomes too great, the valve opens up and tears are released!

Of course, I am not encouraging anyone to weep out of weakness or self-pity. Jesus never cried when he was being criticized, beaten, or crucified! Even so there were still times when Jesus did release his emotions with tears.

Jesus wept when he was moved with compassion for those who mourned the premature death of their friend, Lazarus. (John 11:35)

Jesus wept when he was moved with compassion for the people of Jerusalem who were about to reap the consequences of rejecting their Savior. (Luke 19:41)

Jesus is our example to follow. So if you feel like weeping, do not try to suppress it. Then after you have released your negative emotions with tears, you will find yourself much better able to enjoy the positive emotions of joy and peace.

Psalm 30:5 "Weeping may endure for a night, but joy cometh in the morning."

To mourn is to feel or to express sorrow over a loss or misfortune. Well-meaning friends may try to stop you, but your best friend is the one who just listens. And it is even more comforting if your friend has also experienced a similar loss, so he or she knows exactly how you feel.

Mourning is the normal way that God intended for us to be emotionally healed from the emotion of grief. Jesus said, "Blessed are they that mourn, for they shall be comforted. " (Matthew 5:3)

If you are still grieving over your loss, feel free to share your innermost feelings with Jesus. He knows how you feel, for he has "borne our griefs and carried our sorrows." (Isaiah 53:4)

A loss is forever a loss, but grief does not last forever.

You should also make an effort to do new things. The complete healing from grief is a gradual process that takes time, but doing new and interesting things with others will help you get over your grief much more quickly.

Familiar objects, places, or memories may occasionally reactivate your emotions, but grief essentially ends when you have accepted your situation as it is, and not as you would like it to be.

And the acceptance of your situation becomes complete when you surrender your life fully unto our loving Lord, Jesus Christ, for God is able to work good out of every situation.

While you are experiencing your own grief, it is v easy to be selfishly focused upon your own problems, and forget that your friends, relatives, and immediate members of your own family are also being affected by your divorce.

The children of divorced parents are especially vulnerable. If you have young children, you should make it your top priority to spend quality time with them so they can share their innermost feelings.

Children are the innocent victims of divorce, and often do not understand their own feelings. It is not unusual for them to think that somehow they must have done something to cause their parent's divorce.

Once you have assured them that it was not their fault, they will still want to know why it happened. When you explain this to them, try to be fair and impartial. Encourage them to continue to obey and honor both parents. Do not make them take sides by portraying the other parent as an evil monster.

Ephesians 6:2-3 "Honor thy father and mother, which is the first commandment with promise, that it may be well with thee, and thou mayest live long on the earth.

They also may feel that God has let them down because he did not stop the divorce. Formerly obedient children may even become rebellious. They need to be reminded that God is on their side and that he also hates divorce. Instead of turning away from God, they should be encouraged to turn towards God, for he still hears and answers prayer!

GRIEF AND HOPE

Most people go through five stages of grief. First there is denial, then anger, then depression, then resolution, and then acceptance. Although the negative emotions of anger and depression usually accompany grief, they really do not have to be a part of it.

- Anger is a strong feeling of displeasure that is caused by real or imagined injustice.
- Depression is a continuous state of sadness that is accompanied by feelings of hopelessness and despair.

Depression is often described as "anger turned inward" because it is almost always caused by suppressed anger. In the early stages, a person may switch back and forth from angry outbursts to passive depression, and from passive depression to angry outbursts.

While the anger is openly expressed, the person no longer feels depressed. But when the anger is again suppressed, then the depression gradually returns. The venting of the anger will not provide a permanent cure for the depression, and the suppression of the anger will only lead back into depression again.

This cycle can be expected to continue until the root cause of the anger is resolved. And if this is not done within a reasonable length of time, the person may lose hope and lapse into a permanent state of depression.

When this happens, *hope* must first be restored!

Have you lost the joy that you once had just because of something that has happened to you in the past? I want you to know that there is always hope in God! He is able to set you free from the negative emotions of hopelessness and despair!

Romans 15:13 "May the God of hope fill you with all joy and peace as you trust in him, so that you may overflow with hope by the power of the Holy Spirit. " (New International Version)

It may be comforting for you to know that everyone experiences some form of depression at one time or another. Whenever things do not go the way we think they should, we all tend to become angry. And when there appears to be no solution, we all tend to lose hope and become depressed.

Even the most righteous people in the Bible, like Job, Elijah, and Jeremiah (who was called the "weeping prophet") have become depressed. The unknown writer of the forty-second psalm also suffered from depression, but after he went into the church and prayed, he was able to encourage himself with the following exhortation:

Psalm 42:5 "Why art thou cast down, oh my soul? And why art thou disquieted in me? Hope thou in God, for I shall yet praise him for the help of his countenance."

The psalmist discovered the ultimate cure for depression. He even repeated it three times for emphasis. The cure for depression is *hope* in a loving God, and *faith* in his ability to change your life.

Hope is an expectancy that good will ultimately triumph, and the basis for our hope is God's love and compassion. And when you realize the awesome power of almighty God, then hope gives birth to faith.

Jeremiah 9:24 "But let him that glorieth glory in this, that he understandeth and knoweth me, that I am the Lord who exerciseth loving kindness, judgment, and righteousness in the earth; for in these things I delight, saith the Lord."

And even if you still have some doubt, you can always pray like the man who said, "Lord, I believe, help thou mine unbelief."

Mark 9:23-24 "Jesus said unto him, if thou canst believe, all things are possible to him that believeth. And straightway the father of the child cried out, and said with tears, Lord, I believe, help thou mine unbelief!"

God may use a friend, church pastor, trained counselor, or maybe even a nutritionist or a medical doctor, to help set you free. But your hope and faith should always remain in almighty God, for he is the source of all good things.

Whenever you establish your hope in the goodness of God, and your faith in his ability, you immediately break the curse of depression. And when genuine hope and faith comes in, depression will always leave. Then you are emotionally free to take the next step, which is to deal with any suppressed anger or anything else that may have caused your depression.

ANGER

Anger is a natural response to perceived injustice. The Bible records many times when God was angry, so it cannot be wrong to be angry whenever there is injustice. How-ever, God's anger is always justified, while ours is not.

It may comfort you to know that Jesus was also angry at times. He was angry when he saw how cold and indifferent the Pharisees were to the needs of the man with a paralyzed hand. They did not want Jesus to heal him, because the Law did not allow any "work" on the Sabbath.

Mark 3:5 "And when He [Jesus] had looked round about on them with anger, being grieved for the hardness of their hearts, he saith unto the man, Stretch forth thine hand. And he stretched it out; and his hand was restored as whole as the other."

Even though Jesus was angry, He did not allow it to continue. He released it by taking immediate action to correct the in-justice. He did this by demonstrating to the hardhearted Pharisees that a man's healing was far more important than their legalistic observation of the Sabbath.

It is also reasonable to assume that Jesus was angry when He saw the greedy moneychangers in the temple cheating the faithful worshipers of God.

Matthew 21:12-13 "And Jesus went into the temple of God' and cast out all them that sold and bought in the temple, and overthrew the tables of the money-changers, and the seats of them that sold doves, and said unto them, It is written, My house shall be called the house of prayer, but ye have made it a den of thieves!

In both cases, Jesus was angry over the injustice done to others, but never when it was done to Himself! When He was treated unfairly, He would just commit it to God.

I Peter 2:20-23 "Christ also suffered for us, leaving us an example, that ye should follow His steps; who did no sin, neither was guile found in His mouth; who when He was reviled, reviled not again; when He suffered, He threatened not, but committed himself to Him [God] who judgeth righteously."

We should do the same. However, because of our fallen human nature, we all tend to do just the opposite.

We tend to become angry and want to "get even" whenever injustice is done to ourselves but become very tolerant and forgiving whenever it is done to someone else. And our self-centered anger is often excused as being "righteous anger", when it is really "wrath" or "rage".

- Wrath is anger with the intention to take vengeance upon those causing the injustice.
- Rage is violent anger that is completely out of control and can never be justified.

While it is not wrong to seek justice, only God, who knows the thoughts and intents of all of our hearts, is able to properly execute vengeance.

Romans 12:19-21 "Avenge not yourselves but, rather, give place unto wrath; for it is written, Vengeance is mine; I will repay, saith the Lord! Therefore, if thine enemy hunger, feed him. "... Be not overcome by evil but overcome evil with good!"

Before you can take action to correct any injustice done to you or others, you must first get your anger under control and ask yourself if it is really justified.

Have you been overreacting in anger with God, yourself, your spouse, your children, or maybe even your friends who try to help you?

Have you been overreacting in anger with people just because of some minor inconvenience?

It is perfectly normal to be angry over injustice, but you must always have a good reason! If your anger is "without cause", and really cannot be justified, then you are bringing upon yourself the righteous judgment of God.

Matthew 5:22 "Whosoever is angry with his brother without cause shall be in danger of judgment!"

And even if you do have a good reason to be angry, it will still become a "sin" if you keep it for more than one day.

Ephesians 4:26-27 "Be ye angry, and sin not; let not the sun go down upon your wrath; neither give place to the devil."

Anger is like fresh fruit. At first it can be good for you by motivating you to correct some injustice. But if you keep it too long, it will "spoil" and turn into "wrath!"

James 1:20 "For the wrath of man worketh not the righteousness of God."

No matter how much injustice you may have suffered, (or think you have suffered), you can still be free from all anger even before the day is over. You are probably thinking, "How is it possible to gain control over such a strong emotion in only *one day*?"

The answer is surprisingly simple.

You are cleansed from the sin of unjustified or prolonged anger the same way you are cleansed from any other sin. All you have to do is admit to God that you are angry, and that you need his help to gain control over it. You don't have to do anything else because you are now relying upon the goodness and the faithfulness of God, and not upon your own effort or ability to control your anger.

1 John 1:9 "If we confess our sins, He is faithful and just to forgive us our sins and to cleanse us from all unrighteousness."

As soon as you admit to God that you are angry, and that you need his help to overcome it, the process of inner healing begins. Unless you have developed a deep seated "root of bitterness" (see chapter six), you should find yourself completely free from all anger before the day is over.

While righteous anger is good in that it will motivate you to correct some injustice, it also must be under control. Even if you feel your anger is justified, it should still be confessed as sin if it is not under control. Only then will you be able to take appropriate action and pray for those who caused it.

Another very good reason for not holding on to your anger is that it can destroy your health. It is therefore very important that you become free from all anger as soon as possible.

Our physical bodies were designed by God so that our adrenal glands would activate, our hearts would beat faster and our entire bodies would be energized whenever we are angry or fearful.

This is called the "fight or flight" response and was originally intended by God to provide instant energy and strength to cope with any danger or emergency situations. But if this state is prolonged, then other bodily functions are deprived of their normal energy and nutritional needs.

Prolonged anger will therefore cause the various organs of your body to slow down or malfunction. It suppresses your immune system and cause you to become much more susceptible to various diseases.

Aggression and violence are obviously inappropriate forms of behavior for the release of this extra energy. Until the root cause of your anger is discovered and resolved, a more appropriate response would be to release this energy with some form of physical activity.

And if you are frequently angry over a variety of causes, a regular exercise or sports program would probably be the best long-term solution. This will not only relieve your symptoms, but it will improve your overall health and physical fitness as well.

ROOTS OF ANGER & OVERCOMING

In counseling, people often discover that traumatic experiences which happened in the past are really the root cause or their present anger.

I once read in a newspaper of a young woman who had severely beaten up a burglar. She later admitted that she had just broken up with her boyfriend, and she had taken all her anger out on the burglar. I am sure that she felt much better, but I cannot say the same for the burglar!

You may also discover that the reason you have been overreacting in anger is because of some past experiences. If you think this is your situation, you should ask God to help you honestly search your heart to see if any of these things have been hidden in your subconscious.

- If your anger is justified and under control, then you should pray or take appropriate action to correct whatever had caused it.
- If your anger has been prolonged or unjustified, you should admit to God how you feel, and receive his for-giveness and cleansing.
- If your anger still persists, then you may need to be released from a "root of bitterness" (see chapter six).
- If your anger was caused by severe trauma or is accompanied by other symptoms such as panic attacks, phobias, etc., then you may need individual counseling as well.

After you have gained control over your anger, prayed for those who caused it, and taken action to correct whatever can be changed, you should then accept your present situation as it is, and not as you would like it to be.

Contentment does not come just from having your own way, but rather from accepting the things that you cannot change. Even though the apostle Paul was being unjustly held in a prison, he could still say, "I have learned in whatever state that I am, in this to be content. " (Philippians 4:11)

Of course, acceptance does not mean that you should stop trying to change your situation for the better. I am sure that Paul still sought to be released. It simply means that you should accept your present situation without complaining.

1 Peter 2:20 "For what glory is it if, when ye are buffeted for your faults, ye shall take it patiently? But if ye do well and suffer for it, ye take it patiently, this is acceptable with God."

Reinhold Niebuhr said it so well in the following prayer, The Serenity Prayer:

God grant me the serenity to

Accept the things I cannot change,

The courage to change the things I can,

And the wisdom to know the difference.

CHOOSING DIVORCE

Life is full of choices! God gave us all free will, so what you choose today can drastically affect your future tomorrow.

- Even if you are already in the midst of a divorce, you may still choose to try to save your marriage.
- Even if there has been adultery or sexual perversion, you may still choose to forgive and continue your marriage relationship, providing, of course, that your partner is truly repentant.
- Even if you have already been divorced, you may still choose to restore your marriage, providing, of course, that your partner has not married someone else.

Anyway, before you decide what you want to do, you should first finish reading this book. Then you will know a lot more about what the Bible really does say about marriage, divorce, and remarriage!

In addition, you may want to seek counsel from a pastor or others before you make your final decision. But most important of all, you should seek wisdom from the one who always knows what is your best choice.

That is, of course, from God himself.

James 1:5 "If any of you lack wisdom, let him ask of God, Who giveth to ill men liberally, and upbraideth not, and it shall be given unto him."

The following pages will reveal when you are free to dissolve your marriage with a divorce. But just because you may be morally free to get a divorce, this does not mean that it will always be the best for you and your family.

Many couples have had long and happy marriages after one of them had sincerely repented of his or her sexual immorality.

Many couples have had long and happy marriages after confrontation, legal action, or marital counseling helped put an end to the verbal or physical abuse.

During divorce proceedings, couples still have a lot of interaction with each other, and the reality of separation for life is often not fully comprehended! They become so intent in trying to justify themselves and prove the other person wrong, that they both remain in a form of "denial".

Then, after the divorce eventually becomes final, it is not uncommon for both partners to go into a state of emotional shock when they finally realize that their marriage is over forever. After it is too late, it is not unusual for at least one of the partners to say:

"I wish I had tried harder to save our marriage!"

Don't make the same mistake and wait until it is too late to save your marriage.

A Christian is always morally free to initiate a legal separation or convert existing divorce proceedings into a legal separation. The main advantage of a legal separation over a divorce is that the marriage commitment remains intact. And both partners are encouraged to Work out their marital problems and try to restore their marriage.

"If there is physical abuse, or if you feel your life is in danger, then a legal separation is obviously recommended. And if your spouse is a "fornicator, or covetous, or an idolater, or a railer [someone who violently complains], or a drunkard, or an extortioner, " then you may also want to "put away from yourself that wicked person" by filing for a legal separation. (1 Corinthians 5:9-13)

After a legal separation, neither partner is free to remarry, but all other aspects are very similar to a legal divorce. It is just about as expensive, and the court process is virtually identical.

If you cannot afford the expense, the court can order your spouse to pay the court costs. If neither one of you can afford to pay, then you can always request the assistance of an attorney through Legal Aid.

The judge decides all major issues, such as wife and child support, property settlement, visitation rights, etc. And since most of the decisions have already been made, it can easily be converted into a legal divorce if conditions should ever change.

Can a Christian file for divorce?

Yes, but only when there is sufficient cause. The determination of exactly what are the Biblical grounds for divorce will be clearly defined later in this chapter.

In general, you should not file for a divorce if your spouse has been faithful and is willing to stay with you.

In general, you may file for a divorce if your spouse has been unfaithful or has deserted you.

As previously stated, the act of divorce itself is not a sin. But it would be a sin to file for a divorce if your spouse has been faithful and wants to stay with you. However, if your spouse has already broken your marriage covenant, then it would not be a sin to file for a divorce.

As a matter of fact, getting a divorce may be the most righteous and the best thing that you can do under the circumstances. Joseph was called a "a just man" when he decided to divorce Mary, his betrothed wife. He thought that she had committed adultery, so he was about to file for a private divorce in order to spare her the public humiliation.

Matthew 1:19 "Then Joseph, her husband, being a just man and not willing to make her a public example, was minded to put her away privily [divorce her privately]."

Can a Christian divorce an unbeliever?

Yes, but only under certain conditions.

Although their definitions of an "un- believer" vary, virtually all Christian churches, including the Roman Catholic church, will allow divorce in these cases. This is called the "Pauline Privilege" because the doctrine is based upon the following Scripture written by the apostle Paul:

1 Corinthians 7:15 "But if the unbelieving depart, let him depart. A brother or a sister is not under bondage in such cases; but God has called us to peace."

The original Greek words used here for "under bondage" were also used to denote slavery. If a slave was considered to be no longer "under bondage", he was considered to be free from all previous obligations to his former owner. In like manner, if a married person is considered to be no longer "under bondage", then he or she is free from all marital obligations to his or her former spouse.

However, this does not mean that you can get a divorce just because your partner happens to be an Unbeliever. If there has been no sexual immorality, and your spouse is willing to stay with you, then you are still morally obligated to keep the vows of your marriage covenant.

Corinthians 7:12-13 "If any brother hath a wife that believeth not, and she be pleased to dwell with him, let him not put her away [divorce her]. And the woman who hath a husband that believeth not, and if he be pleased to dwell with her, let her not leave him."

But what about Ezra?

Perhaps you are a very knowledgeable student of the Bible and are wondering whether the historical Book of Ezra indicates that you can file for a divorce even if your unbelieving spouse does not want to leave. But the Bible does not contradict itself, so I will explain.

It is true that God did warn the Israelites not to marry foreign (unbelieving) wives, but he never told them to divorce their foreign wives! There is a big difference between a warning not to marry an unbeliever and being forced to divorce an unbeliever!

The suggestion to divorce all foreign wives was made by a man named Shecaniah, and not by God. Ezra agreed because he thought that this might appease the "fierce wrath of our God." (Ezra 10:14) It was Ezra, and not God, who "made the chief priests, the Levites, and all Israel swear that they should do according to this word. " (Ezra 10:5)

As a priest and a scribe, Ezra should have known better, as the Law of Moses did not allow divorce for this reason. Anyway, the people had to do what they had vowed so they divorced their foreign wives, even though "some of them had wives by whom they had children. " (Ezra 10:44)

Although this was done, there is no indication in the book of Ezra, or anywhere else in the Bible, that it was ever the will of God to divorce unbelieving wives and to separate innocent young children from their parents.

That would be against God's nature.

SPOUSAL ABUSE

Can a Christian divorce an abusive spouse?

Unless you or your children are in danger, then no, not for that reason alone...

My heart goes out to those who have severe marital problems, and especially if there is physical or verbal abuse. Unless there is threat to life, ending your marriage just because of marital problems is like blowing up your car just because it has mechanical problems.

First you should try to fix it.

However, God has called us to peace, so you are always free to file for a legal separation. *And if you are being threatened or physically abused, then this is strongly recommended!*

A temporary separation will not only provide welcome relief from the abuse, but it will also allow time for the abuser to receive counseling.

And whenever there is alcoholism, drug addiction, or physical abuse, there often is also sexual immorality. This includes any forced sexual relations within the marriage as well as adultery outside of the marriage. If this is your situation, you would be free to divorce because of the sexual Immorality.

Desertion, "constructive desertion", or a lengthy Separation with no hope for reunion, may also be sufficient grounds for a divorce. (See chapter five for more on this.) But if reconciliation and reunion is still possible, then you are morally obligated to keep your covenant and seek the restoration of your marriage.

Even though it may be God's will to restore your marriage, this does not mean that you have to "stoically", accept everything that comes your way, and especially if that includes physical or verbal abuse.

The Stoics were an ancient Greek philosophical sect that taught their followers to remain indifferent to their emotions. They were taught to submit passively to every situation, even if it caused pain or harm to their bodies. If you do not value yourself enough to protect yourself from harm, then you are being just like the Stoics.

You have a right to protect yourself from all physical or emotional harm.

When Jesus was about to be crucified, he advised his disciples to buy swords for their protection (Luke 22:36). If you have been threatened and you feel your life may be in danger, you may want to protect yourself by getting a cell phone and buying some chemical mace, an electronic stunning device, or maybe even a firearm.

If your spouse refuses to change or submit to counseling, you can always pray for God to change your spouse and seek help from the outside. There are many public and private agencies that specialize in the treatment of spousal abuse.

The police can make arrests, and courts can issue decrees, but they cannot be with you all of the time. But Jesus Christ is always with you, so you should walk closely with him and spend lots of time in prayer.

What about turning the other cheek?

Sometimes Christians think that they are not supposed to defend themselves because Jesus said, "Whosoever shall smite thee on thy right cheek, turn to him the other also. " (Matthew 5:39)

The world has used this Scripture to portray Christians as being weak and passive, but "turn the other cheek" was never intended to mean that you could not protect yourself. It simply meant that you should not retaliate when insulted. In the Mideast, a single slap on one cheek was considered to be an insult.

A slap on the other cheek was considered to be a greater insult!

And a slap on the mouth was considered to be the greatest insult of all (Acts

23:2). If you study these Scriptures in context, you will find that the overall message is that we should do good and love everyone, even our enemies who may have caused us harm.

Matthew 5:44-45 "Love your enemies, bless them that curse you, do good to them that hate you, and pray for them who despitefully use you, and persecute you, that ye may be children of your Father, who is in heaven.

Although we are to love and pray for those who abuse us, this does not mean that we cannot take corrective action to chasten or punish someone who is being abusive.

Hebrews 12:6-11, "For whom the Lord loveth, he chasteneth, and scourgeth [whips or beats] every son who he receiveth. Now no chastening for the present seemeth to be joyous, but grievous; nevertheless, afterward it yieldeth the peaceable fruit of righteousness unto them who are exercised by it."

We must not be an "enable" of abuse.

Maybe you have done nothing to stop the abuse for fear of retaliation. This is a realistic concern, and it is prudent to take whatever steps you can to protect yourself.

But if you do nothing at all to correct the abuser, then you become an "enabler". In other words, your failure to take any corrective action will "enable" the abusive spouse to continue, and most likely increase, the deviant behavior.

Unless it is dangerous to do so, you should begin by discussing your situation calmly with your spouse. State clearly what you will do if the abuse continues. Then be sure to follow through and do whatever you said you would do.

If verbal confrontation or marriage counseling doesn't work, don't be afraid to use the courts or law enforcement. The civil government was instituted by God for the protection of the innocent and for the "punishment of the evildoers" (1 Peter 2:13-14) "The law is not made for the righteous man, but for the lawless and the disobedient. (1 Timothy 1:9)

Spousal abuse is a crime in most States, and the conviction rate is very high. If criminal charges are filed, the abusive spouse has to appear before a judge. The judge can then order a psychological evaluation and mandatory counseling. In extreme cases, the abuser can be fined and put in jail.

Recently enacted anti-stalking laws and inventions can also help protect victims of physical abuse. Electronic devices can now be attached to the leg of a stalker, and another device can warn the victim if the stalker is in the area.

There are also many private church related services that are available to help victims of domestic violence. You may want to ask your church pastor for information about the services that are available in your local church or community.

If you cannot afford private professional counseling, the city and county governments have free services available. Their services usually include individual or group counseling for both the abuser and the victim.

Most communities also have shelters that can provide emergency housing for extreme situations. However, there is usually a very limited amount of space available, so you may have to provide for your own housing or stay temporarily with a friend or relative.

You can find out what services are provided by your local city or county government by looking in your phone book listings under domestic violence, social services, legal aid, etc. If you cannot find any, you can always call the National Domestic Violence hotline at 1-800-799-SAFE.

Spouse abuse tends to escalate with time, so you should do something about it right away! If you don't do anything at all, then it is most likely to get worse! History has proven that physical and verbal abuse seldom stops without some form of outside intervention.

And before you allow your spouse to return, make sure that there is genuine repentance. If your spouse is truly repentant, there should be either an obvious change in behavior or a willingness to submit to counseling.

If you have been suffering from an abusive relationship, I want you to know that there is hope, for God hears and answers prayer!

Although it is certainly helpful to correct an abuser through verbal confrontation, marriage counseling, court legal actions, or other means, only God can change a person's heart. He does this by giving the person a spiritual rebirth.

The prophets Ezekiel (11:19) and Jeremiah (31:33) were speaking of today's generation when they prophesied to Israel that God was going to remove their 'stony hearts" and "put a new spirit within them", so they could obey His laws.

That "new spirit" is the overcoming Spirit of our Lord Jesus Christ. If the abuser, or anyone else for that matter, will sincerely repent and ask the Spirit of the Lord to come into his or her heart, the Spirit Of the Lord will come in and do a "spiritual heart transplant".

The person then becomes a new creation!

2 Corinthians 5:17-18 "Therefore, if any man be in Christ, he is a new creature; old things are passed away; behold, all things are become new, and all things are of God, who has reconciled unto himself by Jesus Christ!"

This is the first, and the most important step in helping the abuser change the desires of his or her heart. If you or the abuser have never had this personal experience with God, you can find out more about this by turning to the last seven pages of this book.

WHY DO CHRISTIANS CHOOSE DIVORCE?

If all Christians are "new creatures" with "new hearts" and have the Spirit of Christ within them; then why do so many of them still become divorced?

This is a reasonable question, and the answer is as follows:

First, we have to consider the possibility that the person causing the divorce may not even be a true Christian! The person may only be professing Christianity but has never experienced a spiritual rebirth from God. You will know them by their lifestyle for Jesus said, "By their fruits ye shall know them." (Matthew 7:20) In other words, "If it looks like a duck, walks like a duck, and quacks like a duck, then it probably is a duck!"

Secondly, many true Christians have become divorced simply because of their partner's failure to honor their lifetime marriage commitment. He or she may be just an innocent victim, and not at all responsible for the break-up of the marriage.

Thirdly, many true Christians have become divorced because they have yielded to the weaknesses of their carnal nature. We all have free will, so true Christians, and even ministers, priests, evangelists, deacons, deaconesses, teachers, and other church leaders, are not exempt from committing sins that can lead to a divorce.

Although the act of divorce itself is not a sin (see page 36), it is always caused by the sin of at least one of the partners. When the Pharisees objected to the teachings of Jesus by quoting from Moses, Jesus replied, "Moses, because of the hardness of your hearts, suffered you to put away [divorce] your wives; but from the beginning it was not so." (Matthew 19:8)

Here we see that, from the very beginning, divorce has only been allowed by God when people's hearts become hardened by continuous sin. In his letter to the Galatians (5:19-21), the apostle Paul listed seventeen sins which are also the same sins that can destroy marriages.

(1)   Adultery
   • sexual relations outside of marriage
(2)   Fornication
   • any immoral sexual acts
(3)   Uncleanness
   • immoral thoughts or deeds
(4)   Lasciviousness
   • lewd behavior
(5)   Idolatry
   • worship of false gods
(6)   Witchcraft
   • divination, fortune telling, etc.
(7)   Hatred
   • contempt
(8)   Variance
   • untoward criticism or ridicule
(9)   Emulations
   • a superior or demeaning attitude
(10)   Wrath
   • irrational anger; rage
(11)   Strife
   • fighting; defensiveness

(12)   Seditions
- rebellions against authority

(13)   Heresies
- false beliefs

(14)   Envying
- desiring what others have

(15)   Murder
- desire to kill

(16)   Drunkenness
- excessive use of alcohol or other drugs

(17)   Revelings
- riotous or loose carousing

If you are still married and are doing any of these things, then you are the one who is putting your marriage in jeopardy. And, what is even more important, you are also putting your own spiritual relationship with God in jeopardy if you should continue to do such things.

The apostle Paul warned us that those who continue to yield to the desires of their fallen human nature "shall not inherit the kingdom of God!" But those who yield to the Holy Spirit will radiate the wonderful "fruit of the Spirit" in their lives.

Galatians 5:21-23 "As I have also told you in the past, that they who do such things shall not inherit the kingdom ofGod.1 But the fruit of the Spirit is love, joy, peace, long-suffering, gentleness, goodness, faith, meekness, temperance [self-control]."

Perhaps you are wondering how true Christians still sin, and yet, at the same time have the Spirit of Christ abiding in them. In order to understand this, you need to know that there is a difference between the human soul and the human spirit, as confirmed by the following two Scriptures:

1 Thessalonians 5:23, "and I pray God your whole spirit, soul, and body be preserved blameless unto the coming of our Lord Jesus Christ."

Hebrews 4:12 "For the word of God is quick, and powerful, and sharper than any two-edged sword, piercing even to the dividing asunder of soul and spirit."

Your spirit is in the same shape as your physical body (1 Corinthians 15:44), and is the source of your conscience, intuition, and fellowship with God. When you received the Spirit of Christ, your human spirit was "quickened", and your fellowship with God was restored.

Your soul is that part of your spirit nature that expresses your unique human personality. This is the real "you" and includes your conscious and subconscious mind, your free will, and your emotions. When you received the Spirit of Christ, your soul was not immediately changed, but is in the process of being changed into the likeness of Christ.

Your body is obviously your mortal physical form. Your body was not changed when you received the Spirit Of Christ, but it will eventually be changed when it resurrected and "fashioned like his {Jesus) glorious (Philippians 3:21).

Although your body has some involuntary functions, its overall behavior is controlled by your eternal soul.

The proof that your soul is eternal and not part of your body has been attested to by numerous scientific studies on near death experiences.

The proof that your soul controls your body is the fact that embarrassing thoughts will cause you to blush, fearful thoughts will increase your heart rate, and sexual thoughts will stimulate your sex drive.

The reason why true Christians can still sin is because we still have free will, and our souls have not yet been "transformed".

Romans 12:1-2 "I beseech you therefore, brethren, by the mercies of God, that you present your bodies a living sacrifice, holy, acceptable unto God, which is your reasonable service. And be not conformed to this world but be ye transformed by the renewing of your mind, that ye may prove what is that good, and acceptable, and perfect, will of God."

A stubborn, soulish Christian can therefore be just as bad, and do just as much harm, as a non-Christian. The main difference between the two is that the soulish Christian will have a "guilty conscience", while the unbeliever will not.

When the Spirit of God came into your heart, your human spirit was fully restored but not your soul. Your soul is in the process of being "transformed by the renewing of your mind", but this will not be completed until the day you die. Your soul will then be purified from all sin, and only what has been "transformed" to be more like Jesus will remain.

If divorce is the result of sinful behavior, then it can be prevented by living righteously. But we are all sinners, saved by grace, so how can we live righteously?

The answer is that we cannot.

But with the help of the Holy Spirit within us, it is possible to live godly lives. All we have to do is yield to his holy influence and obey his gentle promptings.

Romans 6:15-16 "What then? Shall we sin, because we are not under the law, but under grace? God forbid! Know ye not that to whom ye yield yourselves to obey, his servants ye are whom ye obey, whether of sin unto death, or of obedience unto righteousness?"

Just as you cannot sing like the great Caruso if you do not have the voice, you cannot live godly without God.

We are all born as imperfect beings, so the only way we can remain free from sin is to deny our self-centered soulish lives and continuously yield to our new nature in Christ.

Of course, I realize that marriage is a partnership so if your partner refuses to cooperate, then it may not be possible for you to prevent a divorce. However, if both of you have been spiritually reborn and will submit your lives to the Lordship of Jesus Christ, then your marriage will be filled with God's love and the thought of divorce will not even come to mind.

RESOTRING COMMUNICATION

They say that there are three sides to every divorce. There is his side. There is her side. And then there is the truth!

If your attempts at communication always seem to end up as futile arguments, or if you have to withdraw in order to avoid conflict, then it is quite obvious that there has been a complete breakdown in communication.

The biggest problem in failed or troubled marriages is very often not a lack of love, but a lack of meaningful communication with each other.

Wives often complain that their husbands never listen to them.

Husbands often complain that their wives are always nagging them.

In order to restore communication, you should first make a sincere effort to see the situation from the other person's point of view. Only then can you properly present your own perspective of the situation. The following are three basic rules to help you do this:

1. Listen

- The Bible says that we should all be "swift to hear" and "slow to speak." (James1:19) During heated arguments, people are often so busy trying to defend themselves that they really do not listen to what the other person is saying.

2. Speak Softly

- Speak softly, and don't let the tone of your voice reveal any hidden anger or resentment, for "a soft answer turneth away wrath." (Proverbs 15:1) If you find yourself getting angry, you may have to get alone for a while so that you can pray.

3. Verify

- Make sure that you fully understand what the other person is really saying by repeating in your own words what you think is being said. This gives assurance to the other person that you really do care, and that you really do understand.

In addition to following the three basic rules, you will also improve communication with your spouse if you will:

- Speak only positive words that edify.
- Avoid negative comments, negative condemnation.
- Admit any of your mistakes and be willing to change.

The apostle Paul said it this way:

Ephesians 4:29-32 "Let no corrupt communication proceed from your mouth, but that which is good to the use of edifying, that it may minister grace to the hearers. And grieve not the Holy Spirit of God, by whom you are sealed unto the day of redemption. Let all bitterness, wrath, and anger, and clamor [loud complaining], and evil speaking, be put away from you, with all malice. And be ye kind to one another, tender hearted, forgiving one another, even as God, for Christ's sake hath forgiven you."

FORGIVING AND CORRECTION

Whether your marriage is restored or not, you still have to forgive your spouse for all past offenses. Forgiveness is really not *not* an option if you want to enjoy favor with God and peace of mind.

We are all imperfect human beings, so the key to a happy marriage is not how much you "know", but rather how much you "forget". You do not have to justify or approve of the person's behavior. All you have to do is release that person from the consequences of prior offenses, and then make a firm decision to "forget about it".

Whenever couples have marital strife, they will often bring up each other's past offenses. But God is very "merciful" and, because of Jesus, has agreed to "remember no more!" our sins and iniquities.

Hebrews 8:12 "For I will be merciful to their unrighteousness, and their sins and their iniquities I will remember no more."

Since God has forgiven us and does not bring up our past sins, we should do the same with each other. When we forgive others as we would like to be forgiven, it is just as though the offenses never even happened. Then true love can flourish once more.

Jesus taught us that we should all live by the "Golden Rule" (Luke 6:31), which is to "Do unto others what you would like them to do unto you." If more couples would practice the "Golden Rule" in their marriages, there would be a lot less divorce and a lot more "Golden Anniversaries!"

Whenever we talk about forgiveness, there are always some who think that this means we are supposed to be passive, and that we can never rebuke or punish anyone.

This is simply not true. Love and correction always go together. Even God himself "rebukes", "disciplines", and "punishes" those whom he loves.

Hebrews 12:5-6 "My son, do not make light of the Lord's discipline, and do not lose heart when he rebukes you, because the Lord disciplines those he loves, and he punishes everyone he accepts as a son." (New International Version)

Love is always applicable, but forgiveness is not really applicable if there is no repentance. Jesus indicated that you should first "rebuke" an unrepentant person, and then "if he repents", you should always forgive.

Luke 17:3-4 "If thy brother trespass against thee, rebuke him; and if he repents, forgive him. And if he trespasses against you seventy times in a day, and seventy times in a day turn again to thee, saying I repent; thou shalt forgive him."

And your right to "rebuke" an offender does not justify verbal abuse, nagging, or making demeaning remarks. All correction must be done humbly, "in a spirit of meekness", and never out of anger, wrath, or rage.

Galatians 6:1 "Brethren, if a man be overtaken in a fault, ye which are spiritual restore such a one in the spirit of meekness, considering thyself, lest thou be tempted."

What causes unforgiveness?

The answer may be found in the parable of the prodigal son. (See Luke 15:11-32) Even though the prodigal son had wasted his inheritance, his father immediately forgave him and welcomed him home with great rejoicing.

That is the way that God is!

But when the elder brother found out about this, he was very angry. His reaction to the news reveals that the root cause of his unforgiveness was extreme selfishness. The elder brother was self-centered. All of his world was centered around himself, so he really did not care that his long-lost brother had finally been found safe and sound (15:27).

The elder brother was self-important. He refused to leave the field until his father entreated him (15:28). The elder brother was self-righteous. He extolled his own virtues, and then compared them to the former lifestyle of his younger brother (15:29).

The elder brother was self-seeking. He coveted the attention given to his younger brother and wanted to have it all for himself (15:29-30). The elder brother was self-indulgent. Even though he would inherit twice as much because he was the firstborn, he didn't want his father to share any of it with his impoverished younger brother (15:31).

As Christians, we are all like the prodigal son because our heavenly Father has forgiven us all of our sins and welcomed us back into his family! But if we refuse to forgive others, then we become more like the elder brother, who was very miserable and unhappy.

Jesus taught us in what we call "the Lord's Prayer" that we should pray for God to "forgive us our debts as we forgive our debtors." But then he added the very strong warning that "if ye forgive not men their trespasses, neither will your Father forgive your trespasses." (Matthew 6:9-15)

Jesus also gave us a parable about an unforgiving servant. He said that the kingdom of heaven was like the servant who pleaded with his king for mercy: The servant was unable to pay an extremely large debt, so the king had compassion on him and forgave him the entire debt.

But afterwards, this same servant refused to forgive a fellow servant of an extremely small debt. He even had his fellow servant put into a debtor's prison when he could not pay off his debt.

When the king found out about this, he was very angry. He put the unforgiving servant into the same debtor's prison and turned him over to the "torturers" for punishment until all of the previously forgiven debt was paid in full.

The parable concludes with the very sobering words, "So likewise shall my heavenly Father do also unto you, if you, from your hearts, forgive not everyone his brother his trespasses." (Matthew 18:21-31)

What is the cure for unforgiveness?

Since the root cause of unforgiveness is selfishness, the cure for unforgiveness must be the unselfish love that only comes from God.

But what kind of love? The Bible uses different Greek words to describe love.

The "agape", or godly kind of love, is not the same as the "philo", or friendship kind of love. Affections and friendships may change, but the godly kind of love is never "self-seeking" and "it keeps no records of wrongs".

I Corinthians 13:4-5 "Love [agape] is patient, love is kind. It does not envy, it does not boast, it is not proud. It is not rude, it is not self-seeking, it is not easily angered, it keeps no records of wrongs. " (New International Version)

So how do you get this kind of love?

The answer is that you will receive it when you spend time in God's presence and *dwell in His love!* Then your human love is "made perfect" and it becomes very easy to forgive.

1 John 4:16-17 "God is love, and he that dwelleth in love dwelleth in God, and God in him. Herein is our love made perfect, that we may have boldness in the day of judgment, because as He is, so are we in this world."

However, if you are still unable to forgive your spouse, your former spouse, or anyone else for that matter, then you may have developed a "root of bitterness". This is a more severe condition than unforgiveness, and the way to become free from it will be discussed later in chapter six.

RESTORING MARRIAGE

If you have decided not to divorce, then you are morally obligated to seek the restoration of your marriage, provided, of course, that reunion is still possible. And since God instituted marriage, you will find the way to have a happy and a fulfilled marriage revealed in the Bible.

God created men and women to have different roles in a marriage. The man was given the authority by God to be the head of the family, and the woman was ordained by God to assist him.

1 Corinthians 11:3 "But I would have you know that the head of every man is Christ; and the head of every woman is the man."

Since their roles are different, it should be no surprise to find out that men and women think very differently.

Generally speaking, men seek approval from other people, and especially from their own wives. They feel unfulfilled if they are not loved, respected, and successful.

Generally speaking, women seek very close relationships, especially with their own husbands. They feel unfulfilled if they do not have love, affection, and security.

A happy marriage occurs when the physical and the spiritual needs of both partners are fulfilled. And all of their needs are met when they make Jesus Christ the center of their marriage and live their lives in accordance with His Word.

In divided households, wives should not wait for their husbands to show love before they become submissive. And husbands should not wait for their wives to become submissive before they show love!

In a Christ centered marriage, the wife will encourage and support her husband, dress modestly, and have the inner beauty and strength of a "meek and quiet spirit. " (1 Peter 3:4)

In a Christ centered marriage, the husband will be faithful, love his wife "even as Christ also loved the church" (Ephesians 5:25), protect her, and honor her as an equal heir of eternal life.

1 Peter 3:1-7 "Wives, be in subjection to your own husbands that, if any obey not the word, they may without the word be won by the conversation [lifestyle] of the wives... whose adorning, let it not be that outward adorning of plaiting [braiding] the hair, and of wearing gold, or of putting on of apparel, but let it be the hidden man of the heart in that which is not corruptible, even the ornament of a meek and quiet spirit, which is in the sight of God of great price...

"In like manner, ye husbands, dwell with them according to knowledge, giving honor unto the wife, as unto the weaker vessel, and as being heirs together of the grace of life, that your prayers be not hindered."

First, I want the wives to understand that submission Is only for the sake of order. It does not mean that one person is better than another. The original Greek word (hupotasso) translated here as "subjection" was primarily a military term for setting troops in order.

Submission does not mean that wives cannot minister the Gospel or participate in making family decisions. It only means that the responsibility for making the final decisions has been given to the husband as "the head of the wife."

Ephesians 5:22-23 "Wives, submit yourselves unto your own husbands, as unto the Lord. For the husband is the head of the wife even as Christ is the head of the church."

Submission does not mean blind obedience!

When Peter and the other apostles were told by the high priest not to preach the Gospel, they refused to obey, saying, "We ought to obey God and not man!" (Acts 5:29) If you are asked to do something that you know would not be pleasing to God, then you may, and you should, respectfully refuse to obey.

Colossians 3:18-19 "Wives, submit yourselves unto your own husbands, as it is fit in the Lord. Husbands love your wives and be not bitter against them."

Now I want to speak to the husbands. Have you been bitter towards your wife? Do you realize your prayers will be hindered if you do not love and honor your wife? Did you know there is a big difference between love and lust?

Love seeks the welfare of the other person. Lust seeks only its own self-gratification.

Love gives without demanding anything in return. Lust demands without giving anything in return.

Love that is unfulfilled will bring great sorrow. Lust that is unfulfilled will turn into hate.

It is also very important that you spend time in prayer together with your wife. Just because you have a sexual relationship, does not mean that you have true intimacy. But when you pray together, you share your hearts. Not only do you have greater intimacy, but your prayers of agreement on earth will move the hand of God in heaven.

Matthew 18:19-20 "Again I say unto you, if two or more of you shall agree on earth as touching any thing that they shall ask, it shall be done for them by my Father, who is in heaven. For where two or more are gathered together in my name, there I am in the midst of them."

So, if you want to be loved, respected, and successful in all areas of your life, including your work and your family relationships, then you will have to love your wife; pray in agreement with her; and give her the honor and respect that she is due.

Thirdly, I don't want either of you to become discouraged!

These are the requirements for an ideal marriage, and no marriage is perfect because no human being is perfect. Everyone enters into marriage with at least some unresolved "baggage" that has accumulated from years of past hurts and insecurities.

Nevertheless, a marriage that is very close to this ideal is still attainable if both partners will give their hearts over completely unto the Lord. Only in God is their true peace, love, and security.

And even if you are the only believer in the house, your godly example and testimony may be what will win your partner over to Christ. And if this happens, your partner will be "eternally" grateful. If you are already "born again", but are not living a life pleasing to God, then I strongly urge you to make Jesus your

Lord and not just your Savior. This is even more important today as we draw closer to the "perilous times" that precede the soon return of our Lord Jesus Christ. (2 Timothy 3:1-13)

Matthew 7:21 "Not everyone that saith unto me, Lord, Lord, shall enter into the kingdom of heaven, but he that doeth the will of my Father who is in heaven."

When you obey and do the will of the Father, you not only have a happy and a fulfilled marriage, but you will also have the victorious and the fruitful life that God wants us all to have.

Matthew 7:24-27 "Therefore, whosoever heareth these sayings of mine, and doeth them, I will liken him unto a wise man, who built his house upon a rock. And the rain descended, and the floods came, and the winds blew and beat upon that house, and it fell not, for it was founded upon a rock."

"And everyone that heareth these sayings of mine, and doeth them not, shall be likened unto a foolish man, who built his house upon the sand. And the rains descended, and the came, and the winds blew and beat upon that house, and it fell, great was the fall of it."

If you and your spouse have never really made Jesus the Lord of your lives, then do it now. Then when the tragedies and storms of life attack your household, your marriage will not be shaken, for it is founded upon the rock, Jesus Christ.

4

Adultery is Grounds for Divorce

The seed of adultery, and other forms of sexual immorality begin as tempting thoughts in the mind, but when they are willingly received, they become sin. If they are committed, this will break the marriage covenant and become grounds for divorce.

Jesus taught the truth for the first time in Israel that "whosoever looks upon a woman to lust after her hath committed adultery with her already in his heart." (Matthew 5:28)

He thereby changed the theology of the day from the "letter of the law" to the "spirit of the law." In other words, even when there is no physical contact, the sin of adultery can still occur in a person's mind and heart.

In this Scripture, Jesus was not speaking about the normal and healthy attraction of men and women for each other, nor even of the common sin of sexual lust itself, but specifically of the lustful thoughts that involve a married person.

Since Jesus used the word "adultery", instead of the more inclusive word, "fornication", at least one of the persons involved would have to be married.

Of course, this scripture at least implies that an unmarried man would be committing "fornication" in his heart if he looked lustfully upon an unmarried woman. Sexual acts between unmarried persons are also very serious sins, but the sin of adultery has even greater consequences.

Fornication is defined as any immoral sexual act, and this includes adultery and sexual relations with unmarried persons.

Adultery is defined as sexual intercourse by a married person with someone other than the person's own husband or wife.

Adultery is not just "cheating", or "having an affair", as the world likes to call it. Adultery is a deliberate, irresponsible act of treachery that does irreparable psychological harm to entire families for a few moments of selfish pleasure.

And what if children are accidentally conceived? Can you imagine the mental anguish of a husband if a DNA test reveals that he is not the father of the child he has been raising? And how do you think the child would feel?

Jesus verified the enormity of this sin when he said, "If your right eye offend thee, pluck it out, and cast it from thee. For it is more profitable for thee that one of thy members should perish, and not thy whole body should be cast into hell!" (Matthew 5:29)

But a literal interpretation of this Scripture would cause the church to become known as "the church of the one eyed!" And the removal of a right eye would not prevent lustful looks from the left eye, so what was Jesus really saying?

Well, the "right eye" was considered at the time to be the most vulnerable in battle, so Jesus used it metaphorically to represent the desires of a person's soul. (See Matthew 6:22-23) In other words, if you should have a lustful thought in your mind, you should quickly "pluck it out" before it causes you to commit the very serious sin of adultery.

The Greek word translated here as "hell" (Gehenna) was both a burial ground and a burning garbage dump located southwest of

Jerusalem. Since the punishment for adultery under the Law of Moses was death by stoning, this could be a reference to a person's physical death and burial.

But Jesus later used the words "everlasting fire" and "hellfire" (Gehenna pur) in a very similar warning (Matthew' 18:8-9). And the apostle John confirmed that all "fornicators" who did not repent, would "have their part in the lake which burneth with fire and brimstone!" (Revelation 21:8). Therefore, Jesus must have also been referring to an eternal spiritual death in hell.

Hell is not just a metaphor for extinction. When Jesus told about the fate of Lazarus and the rich man (Luke 16:1931), He revealed that the tormenting fire of hell begins right after death. The rich man was already being "tormented in this flame" when he asked for someone to warn his five brothers, so his brothers must have still been alive.

Yes, I believe in a literal hell. The Bible declares it and the justice of God demands it. But I also believe I am saved from it because of my faith in Jesus Christ and the assurance of God's Word. However, if you do not have this same assurance, you can still receive it by being spiritually "born again" as explained in the last seven pages of this book.

LUST

What the world calls "being in love" should really be called "being in lust". Unfortunately, the worldly media constantly portrays "love" as a brief sexual encounter and anyone who refrains from it as being either naive or stupid.

Lust may be defined as excessive or inappropriate desires, and it can be for money or power as well. It begins when a person allows tempting thoughts to enter into his or her mind. If they are allowed to continue, they eventually become extreme or perverted desires, and a formerly healthy mind then becomes "a reprobate mind" (See Romans 1:24-28).

A man once tried to justify his lust by telling a preacher that it was just normal because he was "male". The preacher replied, "I realize that you are male, but that doesn't mean you have to act like an ani-male!"

You cannot stop yourself from occasionally thinking immoral thoughts, (we all do!), but you can keep them from taking root in your mind. As the saying goes, "You cannot stop the birds from flying over your head, but you can certainly keep them from making a nest in your hair!"

So how do we do this? An addiction is an accumulation of bad habits, so the cure for an addiction is to replace them with good habits. You obviously cannot stop thinking, so you eliminate immoral thoughts by replacing them with moral thoughts.

Philippians 4:8 Finally, brethren, whatever things are true... honest... just... pure... lovely... of good report... if there be any virtue... praise... think on these things."

Lust has three stages.

James 1:14-15 "Let no man say when he is tempted, I am tempted of God; for God cannot be tempted by evil, neither tempeth He any man; but every man is tempted ill when he is drawn away by his own lust and enticed. Then when lust has conceived, it bringeth forth sin; and sin, when it is finished, bringeth forth death."

The first stage is temptation.

All human beings are subject to temptation, but it is not a sin to be tempted with lust. As a man, Jesus was also subject to temptation, but he never allowed it to become sin.

Hebrews 4:15 "For have we not a high priest [Jesus] who cannot be touched with the feeling of our infirmities, but was in all points tempted like as we are, yet without sin."

The second stage is the conception of sin.

Whenever inappropriate or excessive sexual desires are knowingly and willingly received, a spiritual conception takes place, and the dark seed of sin is planted in the person's soul.

The third stage is spiritual death.

Once a sin has been planted in a person's heart, if it is not quickly removed through repentance and confession, it will eventually lead into spiritual death. Whenever a person willingly and knowingly accepts sinful thoughts without any guilt or remorse, then spiritual death has come unto that person's soul.

I have heard well-meaning Christians (and some pastors) say that adulterous thoughts in the heart are "the same as" committing actual acts of adultery. Then they usually admit to having their own lustful thoughts, and say they are "just as guilty" as someone who actually commits adultery.

This all sounds very "humble" and "religious", but it is a deception that tends to justify adultery! Lustful thoughts in the heart are still sins, but they are certainly lesser sins than those that are actually committed. Jesus confirmed that some sins were "greater" than others when he said to Pilate, "He that delivered me unto thee hath the greater sin. " (John 19:11)

No one ever "accidentally" commits adultery. Immoral thoughts will come and go, but acts of adultery are much greater sins because they are always the result of deliberate and willful decisions.

Acts of adultery, homosexuality, lesbianism, bestiality, prostitution, exhibition-ism, child molestation, and other forms of sexual perversion, are deliberate and willful violations of a couple's mutually agreed marriage covenant, so they are considered sufficient grounds for a divorce.

And while immoral thoughts are still hidden in the heart, they will certainly "defile a man " (Matthew 15:19-21), and they may even cause marriage problems, but they are still not grounds for a divorce. But when the immoral sexual acts are *actually committed*, this will not only bring spiritual death to the person's soul, but also to the marriage union as well.

GROUNDS FOR DIVORCE

The Biblical requirements for divorce were first written down by Moses during the Exodus around 1446 BC, and the main

Scripture pertaining to divorce was recorded as follows:

Deuteronomy 24:1 "When a man hath taken a wife, and married her, and it comes to pass that she find no favor in his eyes because he hath found some uncleanness [sexual immorality] in her; then let him write her a bill of divorcement, and give it in her hand, and send her out of the house."

The Hebrew words "ervah-dabar" that are translated here as "uncleanness" can also be translated as "sexual immorality". The word "dabar" means "to lead forth", and the word "ervah" is translated elsewhere in the Bible, fifty-one times, as "nakedness" and once as "shame". Strong's and Young's concordances both define "ervah" as "nudity, nakedness, or shame."

Today, many Hebrew scholars agree that the words "ervah-daber" were originally intended to be a general reference to sexual immorality. This was also confirmed by the teachings of Jesus as indicated in the following two Scriptures:

Matthew 5:31-32 "It hath been said, whosoever shall put away his wife, let him give her a writing of divorcement, but I say unto you that whosoever shall put away his wife, except for the cause of fornication [sexual immorality], causeth her to commit adultery; and whosoever shall marry her that is divorced commiteth adultery."

Matthew 19:3-9 "The Pharisees also came unto Him tempting Him and saying unto Him, 'Is it lawful [according to Mosaic Lawl for a man to put away [divorce] his wife for cause?' And He answered and said unto them, 'Whosoever shall put away [divorce] his wife, except it be for fornication [sexual immorality], and shall marry another, committeth adultery; and whosoever marrieth her who is put away [divorced] doth commit adultery."

The Pharisees had asked Jesus what constituted a "lawful" divorce because this was a very debatable issue at the time. The liberal theological school of Hillel allowed divorce for almost any cause, but the conservative theological school of Shammai only allowed divorce when it was caused by adultery.

Jesus answered their question by saying in effect that, according to the Law of Moses, all of their divorces were invalid "except" when they were caused by "fornication". His use of the all-inclusive word, "fornication", confirmed that the Hebrew words "ervah-dabar" in Deuteronomy 24:1 were originally intended to allow divorce whenever the cause was any form of 'sexual immorality'.

Jesus did not specifically mention adultery, homosexuality, or bestiality, because the word 'fornication' includes those acts, and because the Law of Moses already required that those who committed such acts be put to death.

In practice, however, the death penalty was not enforced because no one was allowed "to put any to death" (John 18:31) without permission from the Roman Court. That is why the theological school of Shammai was able to conclude (erroneously) that adultery was the only valid cause for a divorce.

Sexual immorality is grounds for divorce because it breaks and nullifies the couple's marriage contract.

Marriage is also a legally binding contract and is therefore subject to the laws of secular government. From a purely legal and technical sense, any engagement in extramarital sexual relations is a "breach of contract" because it breaks the mutually agreed terms of the marriage contract.

In the secular business world, if one or both partners do not abide by the conditions of their contract, then the contract is considered to be null and void. Then either partner can petition a civil court to legally dissolve their business partnership.

It is the same way with a marriage contract. If one or both partners do not abide by the conditions of their marriage contract, then the contract is considered to be null and void. Then either partner can petition a civil court to legally dissolve their marriage partnership.

A legal written divorce then satisfies both secular and spiritual laws.

The secular requirements are satisfied because the legal written divorce confirms the dissolution of the marriage contract in accordance with civil laws.

The spiritual requirements are satisfied because the dissolution of the marriage is confirmed by a written divorce in accordance with Mosaic Laws.

Sexual immorality is also grounds for divorce because it breaks and nullifies the couple's marriage vows.

When Jesus revealed that it would be an act of adultery to remarry after a divorce not caused by sexual immorality, he also affirmed that it would *not* be an act of adultery to remarry if the divorce *was* caused by sexual immorality! (See chapter five for more on this.)

Matthew 19:9 "Whosoever shall put away [divorce] his wife, except it be for fornication [sexual immorality], and shall marry another, committeth adultery."

Think about this… if sexual intercourse with another person is not considered to be an act of adultery, then the previous marriage vows must be no longer binding!

Thus, it *must* be the sexual immorality that made the marriage vows no longer binding because the written divorce was unable to do so in the other case when there was no sexual immorality!

Since the marriage vows that had once united them have been broken and are no longer binding, the couple are no longer considered by God to be united as "one flesh". And since their marriage vows were nullified by the sexual immorality, the couple are now free to file for a divorce and permanently separate from each other.

SIN AND GRACE

Do I have to take my spouse back after they cheated?

No way! Even if there is true repentance, you still do not have to take your spouse back. The sexual immorality has broken and nullified your marriage vows, and you are under no moral obligation to renew them.

Don't confuse the taking back of your spouse with the forgiveness of your spouse. You do have to forgive, but the restoration of your marriage is a separate decision.

However, if you would still like to take your spouse back, you may, of course, do so. As a unique illustration of God's continued love for unfaithful Israel, the prophet Hosea was told to marry an adulteress named Gomer. Most Bible scholars believe she was his former wife.

Hosea 3:1-3 "Then the Lord said unto me, Go yet, love a woman beloved of her friend, yet an adulteress, according to the love of the Lord toward the children of Israel, who look to other gods, and love flagons of wine... And I said unto her, thou shalt abide for me many days; thou shalt not play the harlot, and thou shalt not be for another man, so will I also be for thee."

If your spouse, or former spouse, has been unfaithful, then your marriage's prior vows have already been broken, so you should make your decision whether or not to renew them just as if you were getting married for the first time.

In addition, you should consider the possibility that you might acquire some sexually transmitted ailments because of your partner's prior sexual activities...

Some medical testing and/or a further investigation of your former partner's recent sexual history before you make that decision would therefore be very wise.

If both of you are in agreement that you would like to make a new marriage commitment, then I strongly recommend that it be done publicly, with the exchange of vows before witnesses as it was done before. Of course, if you have already been legally divorced, then a new ceremony would also be required by secular laws.

If you are concerned about others knowing about the sexual immorality, you could make it a small private ceremony with just a few friends who already know.

Another way that you could do this discreetly is by "renewing your vows" in a formal church ceremony. Most pastors already do this for happily married couples who just want to express their continued love for each other.

Whether you prefer a small private ceremony, or a public church ceremony, is really up to you. The important thing is that your new lifetime commitment of marital fidelity should be made before God in the presence of witnesses.

This serious and formal commitment before God and others, will not only re-establish the vows of your marriage covenant relationship, but it will also help to prevent any future unfaithfulness.

And the realization that you are not obligated to take your spouse back, should help keep your wayward partner from even "thinking" about being unfaithful again!

God loves the sinner.

God hates the sin but loves the sinner.

If you are the one who committed the sexual acts that brought spiritual death to your marriage, I want you to know that God still loves you, and his mercy and grace is freely given. He will forgive and cleanse you from all unrighteousness, but only if you have sincerely repented of your immoral behavior.

Sexual acts outside of marriage are extremely serious sins and a treacherous betrayal of marital trust. Under the Law of Moses, those who committed acts of adultery, homosexuality, or bestiality, were even put to death!

Leviticus 20:10 "And the man who committeth adultery with another man's wife, even he who committeth adultery with his neighbor's wife, the adulterer and the adulteress shall surely be put to death."

Leviticus 20:13 "If a man also lie with mankind, as he lieth with a woman, both of them have committed an abomination; they shall surely be put to death; their blood be upon them!"

Leviticus 20:15-16 "And if a man lie with a beast, he shall surely be put to death; and ye shall slay the beast! And if a woman approach unto any beast, and lie down thereto, thou shalt kill the and the beast: they shall surely be put to death; their blood upon them!"

You should be thankful that we are now living under and a much better covenant! Jesus Christ has taken upon Himself the just punishment for all our sins. This, of course, includes the death penalty for adultery, bestiality, and homosexuality.

Grace is free, but trust is earned.

Even if you have sincerely repented of your sexual sins and God has forgiven you, it will take time before your spouse will be able to really trust you again. The grace of God is free, but your partner's trust will still have to be earned by your good behavior.

If you are a Christian, it is also important to refrain from sexual sins because your body is now God's temple:

1 Corinthians 6:18-19 "Flee from sexual immorality. All other sins a man commits are outside of his body, but he who sins sexually, sins against his own body. Do you not know that your body is the temple of the Holy Spirit, who is in you, whom you have received from God?" (New International Version)

However, if you should refuse to stop your immoral behavior, I want you to know it will only be a matter of time before you will reap the consequences. Don't think you have escaped the judgment of God just because you seem to be "getting away with it". The judgment of God is often delayed, but only to allow time for true repentance.

Revelation 2:21-22 "And I gave her space to repent of her fornication, and she repented not. Behold, I will cast her into a bed [afflict her with disease], and them that commit adultery with her into great tribulation, except they repent of their deeds!"

If you have never done this before, then do it now: Repent and confess your sexual sins unto God! If you are sincere, God will forgive you and you will never have to suffer the consequences of His righteous judgment.

DESIRE AND GUILT

What if I still have lustful desires?

First, even if you still do have lustful desires, you can, and should, make a firm decision not to commit any more immoral sexual acts. This is a decision that you can make as an act of your own free will, and it is not dependent upon your personal desires. If you are unable to do this, you should see a counselor right away.

Secondly, as much as possible, you should avoid any persons, situations, or things, that would stimulate those desires, such as pornographic magazines, movies, or videos. After all, you wouldn't expect a recovering alcoholic to rent a room over a bar.

Thirdly, you should begin the process of renewing your mind by reading and studying the Bible, regularly attending church, and by seeking fellowship with Christians who are already living godly lives.

Fourthly, and most important, you should seek, praise, and worship Jesus, our Savior and High Priest. He was once a man, and He understands our human weaknesses.

Hebrews 4:15 "For have we not a high priest who cannot be touched with the feeling of our infirmities but was in all points tempted like as we are, yet without sin."

The woman caught in the act of adultery was forgiven, but she was also warned to "Go, and sin no more." (John 8:11)

It is good when an adulterer is forgiven, but it is even better when an adulterer does not even want to sin anymore.

You don't have to suffer from a guilty conscience.

It almost sounds too good to be true, but the Bible reveals that, no matter what you may have done in the past, you can still be completely free from all feelings of guilt. You will, of course, regret the harm you have done to others, but you do not have to suffer from a guilty conscience because God has cleansed your heart.

Hebrews 10:19-22 "Therefore, brothers, since we have confidence to enter the Most Holy Place by the blood of Jesus... Let us draw near to God with a sincere heart in full assurance of faith, having our hearts sprinkled to cleanse us from a guilty conscience." (New International Version)

Once a year, on the Day of Atonement, the High Priest used to sprinkle the blood of animals upon the mercy seat and upon the floor in front of the Ark of God. The "sprinkling of our hearts" is a figurative way of saying that, under the New Covenant, the atoning blood of Jesus Christ cleanses our hearts from a guilty conscience.

Before Jesus came, the blood of animals was used as a substitute to temporarily "cover" the sins of the people. Now, the atoning blood of Jesus permanently "removes our sins." (Luke 24:47)

Before Jesus came, the High Priest could only approach God once each year after a ritual cleansing. Now, Jesus is our High Priest, and we can freely enter into the presence of God anytime. (Hebrews 4:16)

However, if you have not yet sincerely repented, and are continuing to do the same sins, then you will, of course, continue to suffer from a guilty conscience. And even the supreme sacrifice of Jesus Christ cannot protect you from the judgment of God for deliberate and willful sins.

Hebrews 10: 26-27 "For if we sin willfully after we have received the knowledge of the truth, there remaineth no more sacrifice for sins, but a certain fearful looking for of judgment and for indignation, which shall devour the adversaries."

Willful sin is sin that is done intentionally and with full knowledge of the truth. We are all imperfect, and we all sin, but we do not all continue to do the same sins "after we have received the knowledge of the truth."

In order to be completely free from all feelings of guilt, you should also make restitution whenever this is applicable. If you have stolen anything, you should immediately return it. If you have caused anyone injury or loss, then you should be willing to compensate them for that loss.

Numbers 5:5-7 "When a man or woman wrongs another in a way, and so is unfaithful to the Lord, that person is guilty and must confess the sin he has committed. He must [also] make full restitution for his wrong, add one fifth to it, and give it all to the person he has wronged. " (New International Version)

Even if restitution should be impossible, such as with adultery or other sexual sins, you can still apologize and remain faithful from then on. Repentance and confession will set you free from the Judgment of God, but apologizing and making restitution helps to set you free from the judgment of men.

Even if you have repented and apologized, there are always some who will never forgive you for what you have done. This is especially true if that includes adultery or other sexual sins.

But God is merciful, and He is always ready to forgive. If you have sincerely repented and applied the blood of Jesus for the forgiveness of your sins, then God sees you as being "holy, unblameable, and unreprovable in his sight."

Colossians 1:21-23 "And you that were sometime alienated and enemies in your mind by wicked works, yet now He hath reconciled in the body of His flesh through death, to present you holy, unblameable, and unreprovable in His sight, if you continue in the faith, grounded and settled, and be not moved away from the hope of the gospel."

If you now rely upon the righteousness of God in Christ and "continue in the faith " and don't intentionally sin, or if you quickly repent and confess it if you do, then God sees you as righteous in Christ and you are free from the bondage of a guilty conscience.

The apostle Paul is a good example of this. He had once caused Christians to be tortured and killed, but he was still able to say to his accusers, "In this do I exercise myself, to have always a conscience void of offense toward God, and toward men. " (Acts 24:16)

Like Paul, we can also "walk in the light" and keep our conscience free from all guilt and condemnation.

1 John 1:7-9 "If we walk in the light, as He is in the light, we have fellowship with one another, and the blood of Jesus Christ, cleanseth us from all sin. If we say that we have no sin, we deceive ourselves, and the truth is not in us. If we confess our sins, He is faithful and just to forgive us our sins, and to cleanse us from all unrighteousness."

5

When You Can Remarry

The general rule is that divorce and remarriage are permitted only when the marriage covenant has already been broken by sexual immorality, or when one partner leaves and there is no hope for reunion.

For clarity and easy reference, I have listed up front the four subtitles in this chapter which summarize when you can remarry. However, this is a very controversial subject, so please do not be hasty and jump to conclusions without reading the entire chapter and seeking the Lord for confirmation.

- You can remarry after a divorce caused by sexual immorality.
- You can remarry if sexual immorality occurs after the divorce.

- You can remarry if your former spouse has remarried.
- You can remarry if you no longer have hope for reunion.

Whenever remarriage after divorce is discussed, is where emotions run high, and traditions run deep, so don't assume any of these statements to be incorrect before you have had a chance to finish reading this chapter. If my subtitles have upset you, then I suggest that you pray and ask God for His wisdom and peace to guide you before proceeding further into this book.

This chapter is devoted only to the unique cases, when remarriage *should* be allowed.

The next chapter will be devoted only to the unique cases, when remarriage *should not* be allowed.

The most violent opposition to remarriage after a divorce usually comes from married persons who are dissatisfied with their own marriages. As church going Christians, they feel "trapped" in their own unhappy marriages, so they become very angry if a divorced person is allowed to remarry and "get away with it."

I know of a person who walked out of the church service just because a Christian man, who had married a divorced Christian woman, was allowed to sit up front with the pastor and the elders. You can imagine what happened later when this same man was being considered for a possible leadership position in the church.

But divorced Christians are not second-class citizens in the kingdom of God, so I hope that you will lay aside any prejudice or preconceived ideas that you might have. Try to keep an open mind as we begin our study with a very brief history of remarriage after divorce.

A BRIEF HISTORY OF REMARRIAGE

Ever since the requirements for divorce and remarriage were first defined in the Law of Moses around 1446 BC, remarriage after a valid divorce has always been permitted. All of the ancient written "bills of divorcement" found by archeologists have always confirmed the right to remarry after divorce.

The "Didache" (also called "The Teachings of the Twelve Apostles") was probably written somewhere between 50 and 110 AD for the instruction of new converts. It contained very detailed requirements for church leaders on morality, water baptism, holy communion, fasting, and prayer. It even specifically warned against the evils of adultery, fornication, and bodily lusts, but it said absolutely nothing *against* the remarriage of divorced Christians.

The church was severely persecuted by the Roman Empire until 313 AD, when the Emperor, Constantine, and his brother-in-law, Licenius, issued the "Edict of Milan". This edict immediately granted religious freedom for all faiths. Although Constantine also worshiped the pagan Sun god and the mother-goddess Cybele, he publicly endorsed Christianity and made it the only "government approved" religion in the Roman Empire.

Church religious laws and property rights were then enforced by Roman civil laws. Edicts against religious freedom were revoked, and seized properties were returned or compensated. Christianity became socially respectable, so church leaders turned their attention away from evangelism, and began to focus on social and moral issues.

The newly formed church hierarchy was composed mostly of wealthy politicians and aristocrats, who were strongly influenced by various fourth century writers. These (un-married) writers promoted the concept that sexual relations were morally impure, even in marriage!

(See chapter two for more on this subject.)

As a result, in 314 AD, the council of Aries passed a resolution (an opinion, not a law) that remarriage should not be allowed after a divorce while a former spouse was still alive. This policy was hastily adopted only one year after religious freedom was granted, and a new "government approved" church hierarchy was formed.

In 325 AD, a futile attempt was made at the First Ecumenical Council at Nice to pass a decree (a mandatory universal church law for all Christians) forbidding church clergy to marry. If passed, the existing married clergy were to abstain from all sexual relations with their spouses. I wonder what their wives had to say about that!

Although it did not pass then, this eventually did become part of the Canon of the Roman Catholic Church during the sixth century. Even unto this day, they still do not allow their clergy to marry. All of their priests and nuns are required to take vows of celibacy before they are allowed to be ordained.

Their theologians seem to ignore the fact that most of the apostles were married, including Peter, whom they claim to be their first Pope!

Some apostles even brought their wives along with them on their missionary journeys! (See Corinthians 9:5, Matthew 8:14, Mark 1:30, and Luke 4:38)

It is interesting to note that the apostle Paul had prophesied earlier that "some will depart from the faith" and would be "forbidding to marry."

1 Timothy 4:3 "Now the [Holy] Spirit speaketh expressly in the latter times, some will depart from the faith, giving heed to seducing spirits, and doctrines of devils... forbidding to marry, and commanding to abstain from meats."

While the single celibate life was certainly recommended by Paul, he offered it only as a voluntary and a flexible option in order to focus more fully on serving our Lord.

The apostle Paul even encouraged marriage for the average person when he said, "to avoid fornication [sexual immorality], let every man have his own wife, and let every woman have her own husband." (1 Corinthians 7:2)

So why shouldn't the clergy also be able to avoid temptation by having their own marriage partners?

Why shouldn't every lawfully divorced man also be able to avoid temptation by having "his own wife"?

Why shouldn't every lawfully divorced woman be able to avoid temptation by having "her own husband"?

Since "every man " and "every woman" are supposed to have this right, why should the clergy and lawfully divorced Christians be excluded?

Don't they have the same sexual desires as anyone else?

Until the beginning of the fourth century, marriage was not considered to be "indissoluble", and the word, "divorce", only meant the complete dissolution of a marriage. In order to differentiate from the original (and true) meaning of divorce, which has always allowed remarriage, this new (and false) definition is called a "non-dissolution divorce".

In a non-dissolution divorce, marriage is supposedly "indissoluble", so a divorced couple is only allowed "separation from bed and board". And since they are still considered to be married, they are not allowed to remarry as long as their former marriage partner is still alive.

This "non-dissolution" definition of divorce was supported by the fourth century writers, Hermas, Justin Martyr, Athenagoras, Tertullian, Clement of Alexandria, and later by

Ambrose and Jerome[3]. At first Augustine also supported it, but he later changed his mind.

This is an impressive list of intellectual writers, but this fourth century redefinition of marriage and divorce was highly theoretical and speculative, as there was absolutely no precedent in either the ancient or current Jewish traditions.

At the end of the fourth century, the Roman Empire divided into two separate provinces. This forced the church to also divide, although the western church in Rome claimed authority over the eastern church in Constantinople.

The church hierarchy in Rome then reaffirmed its definition of divorce at the council of Mileve in 416 AD. But this new and highly theoretical definition of divorce was still being debated, and in 465 AD the council of Vannes allowed remarriage after a divorce caused by adultery.[4]

During the next century, the Eastern portion of the church in Constantinople separated theologically from the western portion in Rome. Since adultery was

---

[3] Putting Asunder, A history of Divorce in Western Society, by Roderick Phillips, Cambridge University Press, 1988, page 20
[4] Putting Asunder, A history of Divorce in Western Society, by Roderick Phillips, Cambridge University Press, 1988, page 20

punishable by death under the Law of Moses, they introduced the concept that remarriage should be allowed because the adultery made the marriage "morally dead". They rejected the theory that marriage was an "indissoluble sacrament" and began to allow divorce and remarriage for a variety of causes.[5] The Western portion of the church still claimed ecclesiastical superiority and reaffirmed its prohibition of remarriage after divorce at the council of Hereford in 673 AD.

Remarriage after a divorce was permitted later at the council of Verberie in 752 AD, but only in the exceptional case when the wife refused to accompany her husband to another country.[6]

From then on, the overall policy of the Western portion of the church in Rome was consistent in its steadfast opposition to remarriage after a divorce, while the Eastern portion remained consistent in allowing remarriage after divorce.

Eventually the Western portion of the church became known as the Roman Catholic Church, and their "dissolution" definition of

---

[5] Evangelical Dictionary of Theology, edited by W.A. Elwell, Baker Book House, Michigan, 1984, page 323
[6] Putting Asunder, A history of Divorce in Western Society, by Roderick Phillips, Cambridge University Press, 1988, page 21

divorce became one of its permanent doctrines. However, the addition of this doctrine to canon law was delayed for centuries because their own theologians could not agree among themselves on what constituted a valid marriage.

The doctrine proclaiming the indissolubility of marriage was therefore not officially added to the canon of the Roman Catholic church until 1563, as part of the Council of Trent decrees. This document reads as follows:

"A valid marriage between baptized persons (matrimonium ratum) that has been consummated cannot be dissolved by any human power, nor by any cause, save death."[7]

The main Scriptures that were used to try to justify this view were 1 Corinthians 7:39 and Romans 7:2, where the apostle Paul said that "the woman who hath a husband is bound by the law to her husband as long as he liveth."

In other words, they declared marriage to be "indissoluble" as long as both partners remained alive! their interpretation cannot be justified for the following reasons:

- Marriage cannot be considered to be "indissoluble" because Moses and

---

[7] New Catholic Encyclopedia, Volume IX, McGraw-Hill, New York, 1967, page 273

Jesus both allowed the dissolution of a marriage whenever there was sexual immorality.

- The phrase, "bound by the law", was nothing more than a general reference to the Law of Moses, which (as was the custom) made no provision for women to divorce their husbands.
- The phrase, "as long as he liveth", was nothing more than a general reference to the lifetime marriage commitment!

Ironically, the verses that follow reveal that Paul was quoting from the Law of Moses only to support his argument *that marriage can be dissolved.*

Romans 7:2-4 "For the woman who hath a husband is bound by the law to her husband as long as he liveth; but if the husband be dead, she is loosed from the law of her husband... Wherefore, my brethren, ye also have become dead to the law by the body of Christ, that ye should be married to an other, even to Him [Jesus] who is raised from the dead."

In other words, the death of Christ has made us figuratively "dead to the law" of the Old Covenant, so that we can enter into a New Covenant with God and be "married to another", namely to Jesus Christ, the Son of God.

The apostle Paul could not have considered marriage to be "indissoluble" because he also wrote what we now call the "Pauline Privilege" that allows remarriage after a divorce (more will be said about this later in this chapter). If you will study these Scriptures in context, you will see that it was never Paul's intention to declare marriage as being "indissoluble" or to forbid remarriage after a valid divorce.

THE TRADITIONS OF MEN

The fourth century "non-dissolution" definition of divorce, and the correlating doctrine of the "indissolubility" of marriage, have since been legalistically enforced for centuries, so they have very deep roots. These doctrines have influenced the sixteenth century Protestant churches as well, so many of these churches today also prohibit remarriage after a divorce if their former spouses are still living.

Can you imagine how many Christians have prayed fervently for God to "take" their former spouses just so they could remarry?

What if God should decide to answer their prayers?

Those churches that believe that marriages can only be dissolved by the death of a spouse have therefore developed extremely complicated, but very liberal, legalistic rules for the "annulment" of marriages.

An annulment is a formal declaration, based upon various technicalities, that the marriage was never valid. The couple are then considered to have been "only living in sin" while they were legally married, so they can then be given official church approval to remarry.

So, is "living in sin" now supposed to be rewarded?

After stating emphatically that marriage be dissolved except by death, they fail to see the hypocrisy using annulments to accomplish the very same thing!

They try to justify their traditions by saying that they do not "dissolve" marriages; they just declare them as being "invalid" from the very beginning. This means that any children conceived during that time would have to be considered as "illegitimate". Who wants that?

Anyway, the Bible indicates that once a marriage covenant has been confirmed by the vows of both partners, it cannot be annulled by man because, "though it be but a man's covenant, yet if it be confirmed, no man disannulleth or addeth to it." (Galatians 3:15)

Another way that remarriage is allowed by the traditional churches that believe in the "indissolubility" of marriage, is called the "Pauline Privilege".

This is a doctrine that is based upon the apostle Paul's letter to the Corinthian church which allowed divorce and remarriage if an unbelieving spouse should "depart". When properly interpreted, this is a valid doctrine, and more will be said about it later in this chapter.

While the "Pauline Privilege" may seem to be the answer when one partner is an unbeliever, it often breaks down because the churches have different opinions as to when a person actually becomes a "believer".

In the Roman Catholic church, it is when a person has been baptized in their church, and it includes infant baptism. In the Evangelical churches, it is when a person receives and confesses Jesus Christ as their personal Savior. In other churches it is when a person becomes a member or believes a certain doctrine.

After the Protestant Reformation during the sixteenth century, the Protestant churches generally adopted a more liberal position, and almost all agreed that adultery and desertion were sufficient grounds for divorce and remarriage.

Martin Luther wrote many letters on the subject, but he refused to draw up specific rules for regulating divorce and remarriage. He preferred to remain flexible and judge each case by its own merits. In practice, however, he did allow divorce, with the right to remarry, in cases where it was caused by adultery, desertion, or the refusal of conjugal rights.

In the case of desertion, Martin Luther would not permit remarriage until he was completely satisfied that there was no longer hope for reunion. I agree with this position and more will be said about this later in this chapter.

All of the major sixteenth century re-formers, including Martin Luther, John Calvin, Huldreich Zwingli, and Philip Melancthon, agreed to the following doctrinal positions:

- Marriage is a covenant and not a sacrament.
- Marriage is not indissoluble.
- Marriage is not inferior to celibacy.
- Marriage annulments are not Biblical.

WHAT DOES THE BIBLE SAY?

Now that you have had your brief church history lesson, let us return to the simplicity of the Gospel!

After you remove all of the confusing and complicated "traditions of men" that have been added throughout decades of church history, you discover that God has always allowed remarriage after a valid divorce!

God has never changed his moral laws. Only the doctrines and the traditions of men have changed.

What was sinful three thousand years ago is still sinful today.

What was moral three thousand years ago is still moral today.

God never changes, so his basic moral precepts can never change!

Malachi 3:6 "I am the Lord, and I change not."

And Jesus Christ never took away the right to remarry after a valid divorce. He just made it clear whether a divorce was valid or not in accordance with the moral laws that were already established by God and written down by Moses.

Matthew 5:17 "Think not that I am come to destroy the law or the prophets; I am not come to destroy, but to fulfill. For verily I say unto you, Till heaven and earth pass, one jot or one tittle shall in no wise pass from the law, till all be fulfilled!"

The right to remarry after a valid divorce was very clearly stated in the Law of Moses. After a woman had been lawfully divorced, it very plainly stated that she could then "go and be another man's wife."

Deuteronomy 24:1-2 "When a man hath taken a wife, and married her, and it come to pass that she find no favor in his eyes, because he hath found some uncleanness in her; then let him write her a bill of divorcement, and give it in her hand, and send her out of his house. And when she is departed out of his house, she may go and be another man's wife."

I really don't know how the right to remarry after a lawful divorce could be made any clearer than that. There is no mention here, or anywhere else in the Bible, about marriage as being "indissoluble."

There is no mention here, or anywhere else in the   Bible, about divorce as being only "separation from bed and board."

There is no mention here, or anywhere else in the Bible, about remarriage as being allowed "only if your former spouse dies."

These doctrines are merely the trad-itions and opinions of men that originated during the fourth century and have since been passed down to all succeeding generations.

Well, let's break free from the false "Traditions of Men", go back to the Bible, and find out what it really does say about remarriage after divorce.

You can remarry after a divorce caused by sexual immorality.

Immoral sexual acts, such as acts of adultery, homosexuality, bestiality, child molestation, etc. are obvious violations of the marriage vows. And since marriage is established and maintained by the vows of a voluntary marriage covenant (see chapter two), it should be obvious that the breaking of that covenant will also terminate the marriage relationship.

It is therefore not an act of adultery to remarry in this case because the immoral sexual acts have already broken the marriage covenant, and thereby "loosed" the couple from their prior vows. The apostle Paul confirmed this fact in the following Scripture:

1 Corinthians 7:27 "Art thou bound [by your covenant] to a wife? Seek not to be loosed. Art thou loosed from a wife?" [ie, by death or by divorce] Seek not a wife. But if thou marry, thou *hast not sinned* and if a virgin marry, she hath not sinned."

Note, the word, "loosed" has to refer to a lawful divorce and not just to the death of a spouse because if it didn't, then the only way a man could "seek to be loosed" would be to seek the murder of his wife...

And since the Law of Moses very clearly states that after being divorced, a woman "may go and be another man's wife" (Deuteronomy 24:2), there really should not be any question about the right to remarry after a valid and lawful divorce that was caused by sexual immorality.

Most Christians will acknowledge that remarriage after a divorce was allowed under the Law of Moses, but many will question whether or not this was changed by the teachings of Jesus.

Well, let's see what Jesus really did say about the right to remarry after a valid divorce:

Matthew 19:3-9 "The Pharisees also came unto him, tempting him, saying unto him, Is it lawful for a man to put away {divorce] his wife for every cause? "And he answered them, Whosoever shall put away [divorce] his wife, except it be for fornication [sexual immorality], and shall marry another, committeth adultery; and whosoever marrieth her that is put away [divorced] committeth adultery."

First, I want to point out that Jesus had already said previously that He came not to destroy the Law, but to fulfill the Law.

(Matthew 5:17-18) Therefore His answer to the Pharisees could not have been an attempt to change the Law of Moses, which already allowed remarriage after a valid divorce. (Deuteronomy 24:2)

Secondly, Jesus was only answering their question as to whether it was "lawful" or not to divorce for any reason. His answer was only to clarify what the Law of Moses had already said about divorce and remarriage.

Up until this time, the religious leaders had assumed that a person could remarry after any divorce, even if it was not a "lawful" divorce. But Jesus went beyond their original question and revealed that some people had unknowingly committed adultery because they had remarried after a divorce that was not "lawful".

The teachings of Jesus on remarriage after divorce may be summarized as follows:

- Jesus taught that remarriage would be an act of adultery if done after an "unlawful" divorce that was not caused by sexual immorality.
- Jesus taught that remarriage would not be an act of adultery if done after a "lawful" divorce that was caused by sexual immorality.

Think about this, for it can mean only one thing:

Not only did Jesus confirm the validity of the rules for divorce and remarriage in the Law of Moses, but He also confirmed the right to remarry after a lawful divorce.

If remarriage by a married person to someone else is not considered to be an act of adultery, then the previous marriage must have been dissolved by the sexual immorality.

It could not have been the written divorce that dissolved the marriage because it was unable to do so in the other case when there was no sexual immorality.

There really can be no other conclusion!

The New Testament and the Old Testament are therefore in complete agreement that remarriage should always be allowed after a divorce that was caused by sexual immorality.

Remarriage is allowed when sexual immorality occurs after a divorce for the same reasons that it is allowed when it occurs before a divorce. Immoral sexual acts will always break and nullify the vows of a marriage covenant no matter when they may occur.

- An "unlawful" divorce will automatically become a "lawful" divorce, and both partners are then legally and morally free to remarry.

- A legal separation can be converted into a "lawful" divorce, and both partners are then legally and morally free to remarry.

Recently enacted "no fault" divorce laws have made it very easy to obtain a divorce or a legal separation, so sexual immorality is often not the cause.

If this is your situation, it may be difficult to verify whether or not there has been any sexual immorality as you no longer live together. Sometimes he or she will admit it, but it is not uncommon for adulterers to lie. So if you are not sure if your former spouse is having a sexual relationship with someone else, then you may need to hire a private detective.

Nevertheless, you are the only one who needs to be satisfied. If you are personally convinced that your spouse has been unfaithful to your marriage vows, then this is all that you need to know to be morally free to remarry.

You can remarry if your former spouse has remarried.

It really should be very obvious that a marriage relationship is over when one of the partners marries someone else. However, there are still a few churches that teach otherwise, so I will give you four Scriptural reasons why you are free to remarry if your former spouse has remarried.

- You are free to remarry because your marriage covenant has been broken.

If your spouse has married someone else, then this obviously breaks the vows of your marriage covenant. And since your marriage was established by a covenant, this act nullifies your prior vows and makes you free to remarry. In addition, marriage is also a legally binding contract, and the breaking of a contract will always make the partner free to enter into a new contract with another person.

- You are free to remarry because a newer covenant supersedes an older covenant.

It is an indisputable fact that you cannot have two monogamous marriage relationships at the same time, so only one can be valid! The Bible indicates that a newer marriage covenant will supersede an older marriage covenant and make it "obsolete".

Hebrews 8:13 "By calling this covenant new, he has made the first one obsolete; and what is obsolete and aging will soon disappear." (New International Version)

There is a false teaching that it is the first marriage covenant that supersedes all others, and that divorced and remarried Christians are therefore living in what they call, "legal adultery". Yes, it is legal, and yes, some second marriages are acts of adultery, but the adultery is not continuously repeated throughout the entire second marriage as these people claim.

The actual act of adultery is the breaking of the first marriage covenant in order to "marry another". It is not the normal sexual relations that follow that new lifetime commitment. (See Matthew 5:32, 19:9, Mark 10:11-12, and Luke 16:18.)

- You are free to remarry because, if you were faithful, your spouse committed adultery by marrying another.

Even if you do not agree that a newer covenant supersedes an older covenant and makes it obsolete, you certainly must agree that, if you have been faithful, it would be an act of adultery for your spouse to marry another. And we already know that remarriage has always been allowed after a divorce caused by adultery.

Matthew 19:9 "Whosoever shall put away his wife, except it be for fornication, and shall marry another, committeth adultery."

So even if both of you were faithful to your marriage vows while you were married, your "unlawful" divorce would automatically become a "lawful" divorce when your former spouse committed adultery by marrying another.

- You are free to remarry because re-union is impossible as long as your former spouse remains married to another.

Reconciliation and reunion are, of course, not even possible if your former spouse continues to stay married to someone else. And, as will be more fully explained later in this chapter, the only reason why remarriage is sometimes prohibited is so the couple can be reunited.

Under the Law of Moses, reunion with the first marriage partner was not allowed even if the second marriage partner had died because she was considered to be "defiled".

Deuteronomy 24:3-4 "... if the latter husband die, who took her [the divorced woman] to be his wife, her former husband, who sent her away, may not take her back again to be his wife, after that she is defiled; for that is an abomination before the Lord."

The reason why the wife was considered to be "defiled", was either because of her prior sexual immorality (which was the only "lawful" cause for divorce), or because of her adultery if she remarried after an "unlawful" divorce.

Nevertheless, even under his Old Covenant, God's love for Israel allowed for an exception to his own rule. Although she was still considered to be "defiled" because of her spiritual adultery, God still wanted her back!

Jeremiah 3:1 "They say, If a man put away [divorce] his wife, and she go from him, and become another man's, shall he return to her again? Shall not that land be greatly polluted? But thou hast played the harlot with many lovers; yet return unto me, saith the Lord."

Anyway, we are now under a New Covenant, so repentant Christians who were once guilty of sexual sins are now forgiven and cleansed by the blood of Jesus. And since they have been cleansed, they are no longer considered "defiled", and the Old Covenant restrictions on remarrying a former spouse no longer apply.

However, even under our New Covenant, the general rules for marriage still apply. There are only two ways that you might possibly become reunited with your former spouse:

- Your former spouse would have to become divorced for legitimate Biblical reasons.

- Your former spouse's second marriage partner would have to die!

But neither one of these ways are God's perfect will, so you should not be praying for either one to happen. And if you should decide to wait for one of these events to happen, you will probably be waiting for the rest of your life.

Even if your former spouse should eventually become free to marry you, it is unlikely that he or she would do so. No offense is intended, but whatever caused the divorce in the first place would most likely prevent any reconciliation.

So rather than cling to such a fragile hope, I believe it would be far better if you would just admit that your prior marriage relationship is over forever and get on with your own life. And since reunion and reconciliation is impossible as long as your former spouse remains married to another, you are free to marry another.

You can remarry if you no longer have hope for reunion… But what about grace?

Up to this point, remarriage has only been allowed after a divorce that was "lawful" according to the Law of Moses. But today we are "not under the law, but under grace!" (Romans 6:14) Because of the sacrifice of Jesus Christ, we have been "delivered from the law", so we can serve God "in the newness of the Spirit, and not in the oldness of the letter." (Romans 7:6)

In other words, we have been set free from the strict "letter" of the law, so we can obey the "Spirit" of the law.

The Law of Moses included moral laws, ceremonial laws, and dietary laws. The punishment for disobeying these laws has already been paid by the sacrifice of Jesus Christ, but the original intent or "Spirit" of these laws still apply today.

Under the Law of Moses:

- Remarriage was allowed after a divorce caused by sexual immorality because this act broke their vows.
- Remarriage was allowed after the death of a spouse because their vows could no longer be fulfilled.

Under the "Spirit" of the Law:

- Remarriage should also be allowed when there is no hope for reunion because their vows can no longer be fulfilled.

You don't have to keep vows that cannot be fulfilled.

In order to have a marriage union, both partners must make a covenant to live together. If one of them later makes it impossible to fulfill their vows, why should the remaining partner be obligated to remain single?

It is quite obvious that a husband and a wife cannot fulfill the conjugal and other obligations of their marriage vows if they are permanently separated from each other, for all practical purposes it would be as if one of them had died.

Desertion, or a lengthy separation with no hope for reunion, are therefore valid reasons for the dissolution of a marriage and the subsequent right to remarry. This also includes "constructive desertion", where vows cannot be fulfilled because of extreme cruelty, insanity, long term imprisonment, or the refusal of conjugal rights.

This, I believe, is the "Spirit" of the law.

If I made a contract with you to shingle the roof of my house, and then my house burned down, you certainly would not try to enforce our contract by putting shingles on the rubble! But if you returned my deposit and voided our contract, that would be the "Spirit of the law".

Marriage is also a legal contract. Whenever a contract cannot be fulfilled, it is considered to be no longer binding. It can then be legally dissolved in a court of law, and both parties are free to enter into a new contract with anyone they wish. Why wouldn't it be the same with the marriage contract?

You may be wondering, "If this is true, then why did Jesus prohibit remarriage after a divorce that was not caused by sexual immorality? And why wouldn't this still apply?

The answer is revealed in Paul's letter to the church:

1 Corinthians 7:10-11 "And unto the married I command, yet not I, but the Lord, let not the wife depart from her husband; but if she depart, let her remain unmarried or be reconciled to her husband• and let not the husband put away [divorce] his wife."

The only reason Paul prohibited remarriage after a wife left her husband, was so the wife could return and "be reconciled to her husband"!

The only reason Jesus prohibited remarriage after an "unlawful divorce", was so that the wife could return and "be reconciled to her husband"!

In both cases, there had been no sexual immorality, so their marriage covenant was still binding.

If the wife should remarry, this would break her prior marriage covenant, and she could never "be reconciled to her husband."

If the husband should divorce her, it would be an "unlawful" divorce and a stumbling block to any future "reconciliation" with his wife.

This is the real reason why Jesus did not always allow remarriage. It was only because reconciliation was still possible in these cases, and not because God wanted to punish divorced people by keeping them single and celibate.

The apostle Paul's instructions are (1) for the wife not to leave; (2) for her not to remarry if she does; and (3) for the husband not to divorce her, all had one purpose in mind. They were all given so that the couple's marriage might be restored.

And since there was no sexual immorality involved and reunion was still possible, the wife was morally bound to keep the vows of her marriage covenant. Therefore, she was given only two choices.

(1) She could return and "be reconciled to her husband."

(2) She could stay single and "remain unmarried."

If you are in a similar situation, then you are also given the same two choices.

However, if you and your spouse have already been separated for a very long time and you no longer have any hope for reconciliation, then you also have a third choice:

(3) You can remarry if you should so desire.

Since there is no hope for reunion and reconciliation with your former spouse, there is no longer any moral reason why you should not be free to marry another.

FIVE EXAMPLES OF REMARRIAGE

Once you understand the real reason why remarriage is sometimes not allowed, it sets you free from the legalistic interpretations that have so long troubled the church. But because this is such a controversial issue, I will take the time to give five examples to prove your right to remarry if you no longer have hope for reunion, even if there has been no sexual immorality.

Example # 1

The first example is obviously valid, but it helps to prove the point.

The marriage covenant between Adam and Eve could have lasted until the end of the age (Genesis 3:22), but it became limited to a lifetime when sin and death entered into the world.

Marriage covenants are now dissolved by the death of a spouse because there is no reasonable hope of bringing them back together again. I said, "no reasonable hope" because the Lord *could* raise the deceased spouse from the dead, just like he did to Lazarus...

Since there is virtually no hope for reunion after the death of a spouse, the surviving spouse is free to remarry, even if there was no sexual immorality.

1 Corinthians 7:39 "The wife is bound by the law as long as her husband lives; but if her husband be dead, she is at liberty to be married to whom she will; only in the Lord."

In the preceding example where one of the partners has died, this clearly ends the marriage relationship. But in some other cases it is not always so clear exactly when, or if, the marriage has ended.

Example #2

This second example is from my own personal life.

When I was eleven years old, my father was "lost at sea". They found the boat, but they never found his body. My mother, who was pregnant at the time with my sister, kept hoping that he would be found.

My father was a good swimmer, so she thought that maybe he made it to shore, or maybe he was picked up by a passing ship, or maybe the accident caused temporary amnesia! (Hope allows for all kinds of explanations)

Years later, I observed her writing on my sister's baby pictures little notes for my father to read. She still had a faint hope that he might someday return...

But there comes a time when there is no longer hope. My father was declared "legally dead" after a certain number of years, but there is no time limit on hope.

My mother did eventually remarry about thirty years later.

Example # 3

A third example is one that occurred during the war in Vietnam. A young man was captured by the Vietnamese and held in a prison.

His wife was informed by the government that her husband's "dog tags" (metal identification plates) were found and his body was presumed to have been burnt up in a helicopter explosion and fire.

Since he was declared legally dead, the wife eventually lost hope for his return and remarried. When the man finally did return, he found that his wife was legally married to another man.

Unfortunate, yes, but these last two examples point out how impossible it is to determine correctly in every case whether the marriage vows are still binding.

In both of these examples, a decision had to be made, even if there was no sexual immorality.

In these kinds of situations, only those involved should make the decision whether or not they should remarry. It would be extremely presumptuous for a pastor, or anyone else, to make such an important decision for them.

Example # 4

The fourth example is a theoretical one to establish the principle.

A Christian man divorced his young teen-age wife, and then left for an unknown foreign country. He was never heard from again, and there was no way that the wife could find him or know what he was doing. The wife, in accordance with God's instructions, did not remarry, hoping that he would change his mind and return.

Let us suppose that the man died one year later, but the wife does not know it. Must she remain unmarried for the rest of her life just because she does not know this? Is she free to remarry only if she finds this out by chance?

The right to remarry should not be dependent upon chance! She should be free to remarry whenever she loses hope in the possible return of her husband, even if there was no sexual immorality.

It is not God's will to keep his people in bondage.

Example # 5

The fifth example is called the "Pauline Privilege" and is based upon the following Scripture.

1 Corinthians 7:15 "But if the unbelieving [spouse] depart, let him depart. A brother or a sister is not under bondage in such cases: but God has called us to peace."

The Greek words translated here as "under bondage" were also used as a legal term for slavery. If a slave was declared to be "not under bondage", this meant he was free from all obligations to his former owner. Therefore, if a spouse was declared to be "not under bondage" this meant he or she was free from all marital obligations to the spouse who "departs".

Roman Catholic, Eastern, and virtually all of the Protestant churches, are in agreement that the original intent of this verse was to allow remarriage in this particular case.

The Greek word translated here as "depart" was used in Matthew 19:6 and Mark 10:9 to signify a "divorce", but was used elsewhere to signify a "separation". Therefore, some church theologians believe it refers to a divorce, and some believe it refers to simple desertion. However, this doesn't really matter today because a legal divorce before remarriage is now required by secular marriage laws.

When the apostle Paul wrote this Epistle, it was common practice for unbelieving Jews to divorce or desert their spouses whenever they became Christians, so there was virtually no hope for reunion in these cases.

Paul acknowledged that Jesus had not given specific instructions for this particular situation, so he gave his own opinion as an apostle, and he allowed the remaining spouse to remarry, even if there was no sexual immorality.

These five examples have been further confirmation that a person is always free to remarry when there is no longer any hope for reunion. If you are in a similar situation, and are thinking about marrying again, you should ask God for the wisdom to make the right decision.

James 1:5 "If any of you lack wisdom, let him ask of God, Who giveth to all men liberally, and upbraideth not, and it shall be given unto him."

6

When You Should Not Remarry

The general rule is that you should not remarry if the vows of your marriage covenant have never been broken by sexual immorality or by desertion.

In this chapter the following is assumed:

- There has been no sexual immorality before or after your divorce.
- There is at least a possibility that your former marriage can be restored.

In our present time, any limitation of our right to remarry is sometimes considered to be a curse and not a blessing. But these restrictions were given to help prevent frivolous divorces and to restore troubled marriages.

The commandments of God and the teachings of Jesus were not given to condemn us, for without Christ we were condemned already. They were given for our benefit so we Would know how to live more abundant and fruitful lives.

John 10:10 "The thief cometh not but to steal, and to kill, and to destroy; I am come that they might have life, and that they might have it more abundantly."

It simply does not matter whether your divorce was before or after your conversion. When you are converted, your past sins are forgiven, but your marital status still remains the same. The rules and principles of marriage were ordained by God from the very beginning, so they will always remain the same.

1 Corinthians 7:20-27 "Each one should remain in the situation which he was in when God called him… Are you married? Do not seek a divorce. Are you unmarried? Do not seek a wife." (New International Version)

If you were divorced for legitimate Biblical reasons, and free to remarry before your conversion, then you would still be free to remarry after your conversion.

If you were *not* divorced for legitimate Biblical reasons, and were *not* free to remarry before your conversion, then you would *not* be free to remarry after your conversion.

I am sure you will agree that if you were married before your conversion, you wouldn't expect to become single again just because you converted to Christianity! And if you had a valid divorce before your conversion, you certainly wouldn't expect it to become invalid just because you converted to Christianity.

So why would it be any different if you did not have a Biblically valid divorce and you were still bound by your marriage covenant before your conversion?

If your marriage partner has been faithful and wants to stay with you, or if you do not have a Biblically valid divorce, then you are not free to remarry. This was confirmed by our Lord Jesus Christ in the following four Scriptures, which are the only records that we have on what Jesus actually did say about remarriage after divorce.

In order to help make them easier to understand, I have included a brief synopsis of the reasoning behind each Scripture.

Matthew 5:31-32 "It hath been said, whosoever shall put away [divorce] his wife, let him give her a writing of divorcement, but I say unto you that whosoever shall put away [divorce] his wife, except it be for fornication, causeth her to commit adultery; and whosoever shall marry her that is divorced committeth adultery."

- A man who unlawfully divorces his faithful wife causes her to commit adultery if she should remarry because she is still bound by her first marriage covenant.
- A man who marries an unlawfully divorced woman commits adultery because she is still bound by her first marriage covenant.

Matthew 19:9 "Whosoever shall put away [divorce] his wife, except it be for fornication, and shall marry another, committeth adultery; and whosoever marrieth her which is put away [divorced] doth commit adultery."

- A man who unlawfully divorces his faithful wife and marries another commits adultery because he is still bound by his first marriage covenant.
- A man who marries an unlawfully divorced woman commits adultery because she is still bound by her first marriage covenant.

In the next two Scriptures, there is no mention of the "except for fornication" clause, so sexual faithfulness is therefore assumed. This is a reasonable assumption as adulterers were supposed to be put to death according to the Law of Moses…

Mark 10:11-12 "Whosoever shall put away [divorce] his wife, and marry another, committeth adultery against her. And if a woman shall put away [divorce] her husband and be married to another, she committeth adultery."

- A man who unlawfully divorces his faithful wife and marries another commits adultery because he is still bound by his first marriage covenant.
- A woman who unlawfully divorces her faithful husband and marries another commits adultery because she is still bound by her first marriage covenant.

Since the Jewish customs did not allow a wife to divorce her husband, you may be wondering why Jesus said, "If a woman shall put away [divorce] her husband"? Israel was then under Roman occupation, so a wife could petition a secular Roman court and force her husband give her a religious divorce.

If the husband should refuse to obey the court order, he could be fined or severely punished. A wife could, therefore initiate a divorce by Roman civil law, even though it was not allowed by Jewish religious laws.

Personally, I believe the reason was also because Jesus knew that women were really supposed to have the same rights as men. Although the Law of Moses did not include any provisions for a wife to divorce her husband, neither did it deny her the privilege.

Luke 16:18 "Whosoever putteth away [divorces] his wife, and marrieth another, committeth adultery; and whosoever marrieth her that is put away [divorced] from her husband, committeth adultery."

- A man who unlawfully divorces his wife and marries another commits adultery because he is still bound by his first marriage covenant.
- A man who marries an unlawfully divorced woman commits adultery because she is still bound by her first marriage covenant.

All four Scriptures come to the same conclusion!

As long as your spouse remains faithful and does not want to leave you, it would be an act of adultery if you divorced your spouse and married someone else.

But what if my spouse leaves me?

If you are legally separated or your spouse has left you, your first response should be to try to restore your marriage. This also applies if you had an "unlawful" divorce that was not caused by sexual immorality.

A legal separation is only supposed to be a temporary "cooling off" period so couples can resolve their differences. Therefore, if you have a legal separation or an "unlawful" divorce, you are not free to even "date" anyone else at this time, much less remarry!

1 Corinthians 7:10-11 "And to the married I command, yet not I, but the Lord, let not the wife depart from her husband; but and if she depart [i.e.: separates from her husband], let her remain unmarried, or be reconciled to her husband; and let not the husband put away [divorce] his wife."

The wife who left is told to stay single "or be reconciled to her husband", so their marriage can be restored.

The husband is told not to get a divorce, so they can "be reconciled", and their marriage can be restored.

Unless your covenant should be broken later by sexual immorality, or if you should lose hope for the restoration of your marriage (see chapter five), you are not free to remarry.

You are therefore morally obligated by your own marriage vows to actively seek reconciliation and restoration of your marriage. Don't even "think" of marrying anyone else at this time or it will diminish your attempts at reconciliation.

But what if I already remarried?

Reconciliation with your former spouse is obviously no longer possible if you have remarried. No matter what was the cause of your divorce, you are now legally and morally bound by the vows of your new marriage covenant.

Since you cannot have two monogamous covenants at the same time, only your newer marriage covenant remains valid. The Bible confirms that a newer covenant supersedes an older covenant and makes it "obsolete".

Hebrews 8:13 "By calling this covenant new, he has made the first one obsolete; and what is obsolete and aging will soon disappear." (New International Version)

If there was no sexual immorality and reunion was possible, then your second marriage was an act of adultery. But adultery is not an unforgivable sin. Jesus even forgave a woman caught in the very act of adultery. (See John 8:3-11)

While it is too late to change your marital status, it is never too late to get back into God's mercy and grace. Even if you unknowingly committed adultery by remarrying, you should still confess it as sin.

1 John 1:9 "If we say that we have no sin, we deceive ourselves, and the truth is not in us. If we confess our sins, he is faithful and just to forgive us our sins, and to cleanse us from all unrighteousness."

If this describes your situation, why don't you do that right now? Ask your marriage partner to join you.

Shouldn't we just divorce?

Sorry, but a second marriage covenant is just as binding as a first marriage covenant. Although it may not have been God's will for you to marry, it is now God's will for you to keep the vows of your new marriage covenant.

Even though Joshua was deceived into making a covenant with the Gibeonites, he still had to keep his vows. At first the Gibeonites were supposed to be completely destroyed, but because of their covenant with Israel, God even intervened supernaturally in order to protect them!

Once you have entered into a marriage covenant, you cannot justify the breaking of your vows with lame excuses such as:

"I married the wrong person!"

"I don't love (him or her) anymore!"

"I am in love with someone else!"

"I wasn't a Christian when we married!"

"It was not God's will for us to marry!"

As a matter of fact, the choosing of mates is very often done without seeking God's will, guidance, or approval! God gave us all free will, and he will not take it away even if we should make wrong choices.

But the good news is that God is able to work good out of our bad choices, and he can even bless marriages that began for all the wrong reasons.

The marriage of King David and Bathsheba is an excellent example of how God can even work good out of our bad choices.

Their relationship first began as sexual lust when David saw Bathsheba bathing. He had her brought to his home and they committed adultery while her husband was away. When she conceived his child, he tried to cover up his sin by having her husband killed. Bathsheba then married the murderer of her first husband, and their firstborn son died shortly after birth.

Now that was a pretty bad start for a marriage!

But after they had both sincerely repented for their past sins, a second son named Solomon was born. When he grew up, he became God's chosen king over the entire nation of Israel.

Solomon wrote Psalms 72 and 127, most of Proverbs, and probably Ecclesiastes and Song of Songs. He was also the direct ancestor of Joseph, who was married to Mary, the mother of Jesus, our Lord and Savior.

Now wouldn't you like to have a son like Solomon?

God took a marriage that began as the result of lust, adultery, and murder, and turned it around for good. If you have also entered into a marriage for all the wrong reasons, I want you to know that what God did for David and Bathsheba, *He can also do for you.*

THE ROOT OF BITTERNESS

Sometimes people will say that they don't want to be reconciled with their marriage partners, and you may also feel the same way. However, after in-depth counseling, many discover that the real reason for rejecting their marriage partners is a "root of bitterness" that has developed over many years from an accumulation of offenses that have never been forgiven.

There are others who really do want to be reconciled but have been unable to do so. All attempts at reconciliation seem to end in futile arguments. If this has happened to you, then you also may have a "root of bitterness".

Hebrews 12:14-15 "Follow peace with all men, and holiness, without which no man will see the Lord; looking diligently lest any man fail of the grace of

God, lest any root of bitterness spring up to trouble you, and by it many be defiled."

A "root of bitterness" comes from holding on to negative emotions such as anger, resentment, contempt, jealousy, envy, etc. and it has both physical and emotional symptoms.

If any of these emotions rise up whenever you think or talk about a certain person or incident, then you may have a "root of bitterness".

If you feel your mouth drop and your face stiffen whenever you think or talk about a certain person or incident, then you may have a "root of bitterness"!

Cain was probably the first person to develop a "root of bitterness". When his brother Abel's offering was pleasing to God, and his own was rejected, Cain became very angry and "his countenance fell."

Genesis 4:4-7 "And the Lord had respect unto Abel and to his offering; but unto Cain and to his offering he had not respect. And Cain was very wroth [angry] and his countenance fell. And the Lord said unto Cain, Why art thou wroth? And why is thy countenance fallen? If thou doest well, shalt not thou be accepted? And if thou doest not well, sin lieth at the door. And unto thee shall be his desire, and thou shall rule over him."

God warned Cain that he must quickly get control over his anger before it became a sin. Cain was very angry, but this had not yet become sin for the Lord indicated that it was only lying at the door of his heart.

But Cain refused to let go of his anger.

Then he began to blame his more righteous brother for his own inability to please God. As soon as he tried to justify himself by blaming another, a "root of bitterness" began to form in his heart. Because he refused to repent, his bitterness continued to grow until he eventually fulfilled his irrational desires for revenge by murdering his own brother.

The morals of this Bible story are this:

- Negative emotions can turn into a root of bitterness.
- A root of bitterness begins when you blame others.
- Bitterness eventually causes a desire for revenge.

Whenever bitterness results from a divorce or marital problems, the blame and any desires for revenge are usually directed towards their spouses. Violent arguments, wife beatings, property destruction, and sometimes even murder, are all the result of prolonged and unresolved bitterness.

If a person should blame himself, then any desire for revenge will turn inward. This can result in extreme depression, recklessness, self-hate, and maybe even thoughts of suicide. If a person should blame God, then the revenge is expressed according to whether or not the person fears God.

When a person does not fear God, the desire for revenge may be expressed by blaspheming God, practicing witchcraft, or by unrestrained wickedness.

When a person does fear God, the desire for revenge is suppressed, so the anger turns inward and causes depression and feelings of despair and hopelessness.

The latter was the case with Job. When troubles came, he first suppressed his anger and tried not to blame God. But as his troubles increased, he eventually did blame God. Then he became very depressed when he realized he couldn't do anything about it!

What was God's response?

First, he rebuked Job for speaking so presumptuously. Then he went straight to the heart of the matter, which was that Job was really trying to justify himself by blaming God:

Job 40:8 "Wilt thou condemn me, *that thou* may be justified?

Have you become like Job? Have you been blaming God or others for your troubles in order to justify yourself? If so, then you may have developed a root of bitterness.

First, there is always a loss.

There is always some kind of a loss before a root of bitterness can begin to grow. For Cain it was the loss of his favor with God. For Job it was the loss of his family, his wealth, and his health! For you it could be any number of things, such as the loss of your reputation, finances, security, marital love, family relationships, self-esteem, etc.

Second, there is blame.

If you have a root of bitterness, you will find yourself wanting to blame someone or something for your loss.

You may blame God, your former spouse, your parents, your lawyer, or maybe even your friends who are only trying to help! And if you are unable to blame anyone or anything else, then you may blame yourself for "being so stupid!" However, the latter is only a subtle form of pride because no one is perfect and we all make mistakes.

As a matter of fact, that is why we all need Jesus!

If this describes how you feel, then you may need individual counseling from a church pastor or a professional counselor. But if you are able to see that you, and not anyone else, are really the cause of your own bitterness, then you have taken the first step towards complete recovery.

What causes bitterness?

Everyone suffers from the emotion of grief after a loss, and this is normal, but not everyone becomes bitter after a loss. So what is it that causes some people to become bitter, while others do not, even if they suffer the same loss? If the main difference between grief and bitterness is an overwhelming compulsion to blame someone else, then this must be a major clue as to its root cause.

Well, if you really do have a root of bitterness, you may not want to hear this, but I want you "better" and not "bitter" so I will tell you anyway!

The "root of bitterness" is a self-righteous spirit that rejects the grace of God, and then seeks to be justified by blaming someone else.

This truth may be hard to receive at first, but you can take consolation in the fact that we all struggle at times with pride and self-righteousness. Instead of admitting our own faults, we all have a tendency to blame others for our problems.

Eve did it by blaming the serpent!

Adam did it by blaming Eve!

Saul did it by blaming the people!

I heard a funny story about a man who supposedly saw a devil sitting on the sidewalk, crying his beady little eyes out! The man asked him why he was crying. The devil whimpered, "All those people in that church keep blaming me for all their problems, and I haven't even done a thing!"

Of course, I realize that we "wrestle not against flesh and blood, but against principalities and powers. " (Ephesians 6:12), but the moral of this story is that we should take responsibility for our own actions, and not blame others, even if you believe it is from the devil!

At this point, it is time for you to honestly search your own heart to see if this applies to you. Have you been trying to justify your own failings by blaming others?

Self-righteous people do not want to change or admit any weaknesses, so they will try to justify themselves by blaming others.

Humble people will readily admit their own failings, and they are quick to apologize and offer to make restitution for any harm that they may have done.

The other person may even be at fault, but before you pronounce judgment, Jesus said that you should "first cast the beam out of thine own eye, and then thou shalt see clearly to cast the mote [a small speck] out of thy brother's eye. (Luke 6:42)

Even if you only have a very small speck in your own eye, you will still have to admit your own faults if you want to see clearly! Then if you should have to correct anyone, it will always be done humbly, "in a spirit of meekness, considering thyself, lest thou also be tempted." (Galatians 6:1)

FREEDOM FROM BITTERNESS

How do I get free from bitterness?

I am glad you asked! (Or at least I hope you asked!) One of the signs of humility is to admit your own weaknesses and to seek help from God and others!

The first thing you should do is *stop blaming others* for your own misfortune. This can be done immediately as an act of your free will, and it does not require any change in your attitude.

However, to be completely free from all feelings of bitterness, your attitude will eventually have to change. And since the root cause of bitterness is self-righteousness, the first thing you will have to do is humble yourself.

How do you do that?

You humble yourself by admitting your own weaknesses, and by praying to God for his mercy and strength.

2 Chronicles 7:14 "If my people, who are called by my name, shall humble themselves and pray, and seek my face, and turn from their wicked ways, then I will hear from heaven, and will forgive their sin, and will heal their land."

No man is an island. We all need God and each other.

One of the symptoms of self-righteousness is to think that we do not need any help from anyone, including our Creator. But those who will "humble themselves and pray", and turn away from willful sins, will be forgiven and set free from the bondage of self-righteousness and pride.

In the parable of the Pharisee and the publican, the Pharisee was only exalting himself when he prayed. But the lowly publican (tax collector) humbled himself by confessing his sins and seeking God's mercy and grace.

Luke 18:11-13 "The pharisee stood and prayed thus and said, God, I thank thee that I am not as other men are, extortioners, unjust, adulterers, or even as this publican [tax collector] ... The publican, standing afar off, would not lift up so much as his eyes unto heaven, but smote his breast, saying, God be merciful to me a sinner! I tell you this man went down to his house justified rather than the other; for everyone who exalteth himself shall be abased; and he that humbleth himself shall be exalted."

True humility begins when we acknowledge our own weaknesses and pray for God's mercy and grace.

True humility is a completely honest appraisal of ourselves that includes our weaknesses as well as our strengths.

True humility will draw us closer to God when we realize that we can do absolutely nothing worthwhile without his inspiration and assistance. (John 15:5)

True humility increases as we grow in the knowledge of Jesus Christ and in his humility. (Philippians 2:5-8)

True humility gives us greater appreciation for what Jesus has done for us and for the blessings that we already have received.

Be thankful.

You cannot be bitter and thankful at the same time, so the next step in overcoming a root of bitterness is "an attitude of gratitude" for the goodness, mercy, and grace of God.

1 Thessalonians 5:18 "In everything give thanks, for this is the will of God in Christ Jesus concerning you."

Even if you have lots of problems, you can still be very thankful for the blessings that you already do have. The man with no shoes stopped complaining when he met the man with no feet.

Speak only blessings.

No matter what someone may have done to you in the past, you should still "bless them that curse you, and pray for them who despitefully use you. " (Luke 6:28)

James 3:10 "Out of the same mouth proceed blessing and cursing. My brethren, these things should not be."

And even if your present circumstances do not look good right now, you can still be thankful because you know that "all things work together for good to them that love God." When you are loving and serving God, all of your life experiences, both the good and the bad, help to make you more like Jesus.

Romans 8:28-29 "For we know that all things work together good to them that love God, to them who are the called according to his purpose, for whom he did foreknow, he also did predestinate to be conformed to the image of his Son."

Worship God.

Praise and worship helps to bring you into the presence of God, and this is where you receive the strength and the power to overcome negative emotions.

John 4:23 Jesus said, "But the hour cometh, and now is, when the true worshipers shall worship the Father in spirit and in truth; for the Father seeketh such to worship him."

A good way to describe the progression of our relationship with God is that we first "enter into his gates with thanksgiving, and into his courts with praise." (Psalm 100:4) Then, because of what Jesus has done, we can now enter into his actual presence and "worship the Father in spirit and in truth."

You praise God with your understanding, but you worship God with your emotions.

Praise sets you free from negative confessions.

Worship sets you free from negative emotions.

Worship is love expressed as an emotion. Whether it is in a loud voice or in reverent silence; whether it is in a church or at home; true worship is an intense love and adoration that comes from deep within the heart.

And when you do worship God sincerely and honestly "in spirit and in truth", you partake of his divine nature, and He replaces the negative emotions that once caused bitterness with his positive emotions of love, joy, and peace.

Bitterness disappears when you truly forgive.

After you have humbled yourself by admitting your own faults, prayed for God's mercy and grace; expressed gratitude for what you do have; and praised and worshiped God; you should find it very easy to forgive.

However, if you are still unable to feel a complete release of your emotions right away, do not think you have failed. Forgiveness is often a process that begins as a decision and only becomes complete with time.

And don't confuse any lack of trust with unforgiveness. Trust is based upon the other person's behavior, but forgiveness is based upon the unconditional love of God.

1 John 4:11-12 "Beloved, if God so loved us, we ought also to love one another ... If we love one another, God dwelleth in us, and his love is perfected in us."

Just as there are degrees of love, there are also degrees of forgiveness. You will know that "his love" has been "perfected" in you when you are able to pray for God to forgive even those who have caused you great harm.

Stephen was able to pray for God to forgive those who were stoning him to death, saying, "Lord, lay not this sin to their charge!" (Acts 7:60)

Jesus was able to pray for his Father to forgive those who were crucifying him, saying, "Father, forgive them; for they know not what they do!" (Luke 23:34)

7

Ordaining Divorced Ministers

Divorced and remarried ministers may be ordained into any ministry for which they are qualified. The requirement for a bishop, deacon, or elder to be "the husband of one wife" was intended only to exclude from church leadership those who continued to practice polygamy.

It is almost incomprehensible to me that divorce and remarriage should be singled out as the only so-called sin that will keep a person from ordination into Christian ministry.

It seems to be only common sense that divorced and remarried Christians should be allowed the same privileges of serving our Lord Jesus Christ in ministry that is already allowed those who used to be thieves, murderers, adulterers, fornicators, drug dealers, rapists, gang leaders, and the like.

However, I will try to explain to the reader why so many churches still do not allow divorced and remarried persons to be ordained into Christian ministry. They base their doctrine primarily upon the following letters written by the apostle Paul to the churches:

1 Timothy 3:2-7 "A bishop [episkopos] then must be blameless, the husband of one wife, vigilant, sober, of good behavior, given to hospitality, apt to teach; not given to wine, not a striker, not greedy, of filthy lucre, but patient, not a brawler, not covetous; one that ruleth well his own house, having his children in subjection with all gravity (for if a man know not how to rule his own house, how can he take care of the church of God?) etc."

1 Timothy 3:8-13 "In like manner, must the deacons [diakanos] be grave, not double tongued, not given to much wine, not greedy of filthy lucre, holding the mystery of faith in a pure conscience. And let these also first be proved; then let them use the office of a deacon, being found blameless. Even so must their wives be grave, not slanderers, sober, faithful in all things. Let the deacons [diakanos] be the husbands of one wife, ruling their children and houses well etc."

Titus 1:5-6 "... and ordain elders [presbuteros] in every city as I had appointed thee, if any be blameless, the husband of one wife, having faithful children not accused of riot, or unruly. For a bishop [episkopos] must be blameless, as the steward of God, not self-willed, not soon angry, not given to wine, no striker, not given to filthy lucre etc."

I have included extra verses to show that all these requirements were definitely intended to be qualifications for leadership in the early church, and that being the "husband of one wife" was only one of many requirements.

On this, we all agree. Yet I wonder how many bishops, deacons, and elders who are now refusing to ordain divorced and remarried Christians, would themselves be able to fulfill every one of these requirements for church leadership?

The Greek words for "husband of one wife" can be literally translated as:

"One [mia] woman [gune] man [aner]".

But the Greek language had no words for wife or husband, so this can also be translated as "one wife-husband".

This is where the misunderstanding began.

Because of their preoccupation with celibacy, some fourth century writers and theologians thought that the requirement for leaders to be "the husband of one wife" meant that divorced and remarried Christians could never be ordained as church leaders. Some monks even argued that widowers should also be excluded for the same reason.

Their reasoning appears to be based upon their belief that a "truly spiritual man" should either abstain from all sexual relations or be allowed only a very limited amount of sexual pleasure during his lifetime!

Don't laugh, many people still believe this way today!

The Lord once said to His people, "Come, let us reason together", so let us do that now as I ask you a few questions.

- Is it reasonable to assume that highly qualified divorced and remarried Christians should be forever banned from church leadership?
- Is it reasonable to allow the ordination of married Christians who used to "live together" with someone else, and then reject those who used to be legally married?
- Is it reasonable to assume that the apostle Paul intended to establish (on his own) a completely new doctrine against divorced people without even mentioning the word "divorce"?
- Is it reasonable to assume that Jesus was somehow negligent in that He did not even mention anything about rejecting divorced and remarried persons from ministry?
- Is it reasonable to assume the words "husband of one wife" were intended to exclude divorced and remarried

persons, when they can much more logically be applied to exclude polygamists?

Polygamy is the practice of having more than one husband or wife at the same time. Many Bible scholars today agree that these Scriptures were only intended to exclude polygamists from leadership, and that they have nothing at all to do with remarriage after a divorce.

Nevertheless, many theologians today still claim that these Scriptures were intended to exclude divorced and remarried Christians instead of polygamists. The only reason they can give is that very few people practiced polygamy at that time.

So what difference does that make?

By now you are probably wondering how intelligent, well-intentioned church theologians could have ever come up with such ridiculous conclusions!

I have wondered myself.

Why are divorced and remarried Christians refused ordination?

Religious prejudice is probably the main reason.

The discrimination against divorced and remarried people in ministry first began during the fourth century. At that time the newly formed church hierarchy was very strongly influenced by various writers who believed (1) that divorce was always a sin, (2) that remarriage after divorce was always a sin, and (3) that celibacy was equated with greater spirituality. (See chapter two for more on this.)

But divorce is *not* always a sin because God himself divorced Israel when they committed spiritual adultery. (Jeremiah 3:8)

And remarriage is *not* always a sin because Moses and Jesus both allowed remarriage after a divorce caused by sexual immorality. (Deuteronomy 24:1-2, Matthew 5:32, 19:9)

And celibacy does *not* mean greater spirituality because the apostle Peter (Matthew 8:14), the brothers of Jesus, and most of the other apostles were married. (1 Corinthians 9:5)

If you discount these erroneous beliefs, it becomes very clear that the words "husband of one wife" were intended only to exclude *polygamists* from church leadership and not divorced people. Jesus confirmed that polygamy was never God's will when He said, "at the beginning of creation God 'made them male and female' and the *two* will become one flesh."

Mark 10:6-8 "But at the beginning of creation God made them male and female. For this reason a man will leave his father and mother and be united to his wife, and the *two* will become one flesh. So they are no longer *two*, but one. " (New International Version)

Since this new revelation was given by Jesus to enlighten Jewish scholars who had missed it at up until then, I do not find it at all surprising that the early church leaders would require bishops, deacons, and elders to have only one wife.

Polygamous marriage first began with Lamech, a fifth generation descendent from the wicked Cain. It was probably allowed later under the Law of Moses because it was a lesser evil than the common practice of prostitution. And since birth control devices were not invented yet, polygamy at least prevented the conception of illegitimate children, who would never know their fathers!

Although polygamy is now banned in most countries, it was not illegal when Paul wrote his requirements for church leadership. And even when polygamy was legal, very few practiced it because most men could not afford the extra wives.

King Solomon was very wealthy, so he could afford as many wives as he wanted. Even though the Bible very clearly warned that a king should *not* "multiply wives unto himself" (Deuteronomy 17:17), he disregarded the warning and married 700 wives and 300 concubines!

Can you imagine that?

And yet God never removed Solomon from being King just because of his many wives! And even when he greatly sinned later by following after his wives' pagan gods, he still remained as God's chosen ruler over all Israel.

And God never removed Abraham, Moses, David, or any of the other patriarchs from their leadership positions when they married additional wives.

It is ironic that the patriarchs of old could have as many wives as they wanted, and still keep their leadership positions. While today, if a man should marry just *one* wife after being legally divorced, he is forever banned from all ministry positions in the church.

It just doesn't make sense!

It gets even more ridiculous when you realize that in most churches today, a man could murder his wife, repent, remarry, and then be ordained into any ministry position that is available. But the man who legally and lawfully divorces his unfaithful wife and marries another, is forever rejected from all church leadership!

Does this mean it is better to murder your wife?

The apparent conclusion of traditional church theology is that remarrying after a divorce must be a much greater sin than murdering your spouse.

Need I say anymore?

JUDAIC LAW & PRIESTLY REMARRIAGE

Another cause of the prejudice and discrimination against divorced and remarried Christians is the misunderstanding of why priests under the Old Covenant were not allowed to marry divorced women.

Leviticus 21:7 "They [the priests] shall not take a wife who is a whore [prostitute], or profane; neither shall they take a woman put away [divorced] from her husband; for he is holy unto his God."

The first thing that you need to know is that only women could be divorced at this time. As with the Greeks and the Romans, even if a man had sexual relations outside of marriage, he still could not be divorced by his wife.

The second thing that you need to know is that sexual immorality was the only legitimate cause for a divorce according to the Law of Moses.

Deuteronomy 24:1 "And if it come to pass that she find no favor in his eyes, because he has found some uncleanness [sexual immorality] in her; then let him write her a bill of divorcement."

When you put these two facts together, this means that, if the accusations, were true, *then every divorced woman was guilty of sexual immorality.*

This is the real reason why Jewish priests were not allowed to marry divorced women. It was because a divorced woman would be likely to continue her sexual immorality, and not just because she happened to be divorced!

The standards of holiness were even stricter for a high priest. He was not only forbidden to marry a divorced woman, but he also had to be free from all physical imperfections and could only marry a virgin. (Leviticus 21:13) But now we are under a new and a much better covenant with God, and Jesus Christ is our high priest.

Hebrews 4:15 "Seeing then that we have a great high priest, that is passed into the heavens, Jesus, the Son of God, let us hold fast our profession. For we have not a high priest who cannot be touched with the feeling of our infirmities, but was in all points tempted like as we are, yet without sin. Let us, therefore, come boldly unto the throne of grace, that we may obtain mercy, and find grace to help in time of need."

Even if you once did live an immoral life in the past, under our New Covenant of grace, you can now confess your sins unto God and the sacrificial blood of Jesus Christ, our high priest, will cleanse you from all of your sins.

And the legal systems are completely different today. Women can now divorce men, and secular judges allow divorce for a variety of reasons other than sexual immorality. Therefore, not all divorced persons today have been guilty of any sexual misconduct.

If the Old Covenant qualifications for the priesthood were applied to the present day clergy, this would now condemn the innocent along with the guilty and disqualify all those whom Jesus Christ has redeemed.

Another aspect of the prejudice against those who have remarried after a divorce is the unalterable permanency of the discrimination against them. No other sins, or presumed sins, carry stigmas that last for a lifetime.

All of the other requirements for offices in the church can be met with genuine repentance, but how can you repent of "being" a divorced person? You can repent of any sins that may have caused the divorce, but it is impossible to change what has already happened.

After his resurrection, Jesus told his disciples that they should preach "repentance and remission of sins" in his name:

Luke 24:46-47 "And He [Jesus] said unto them, Thus it is written, and thus it behooved Christ to suffer, and to rise from the dead the third day; and that repentance and remission of sins should be preached in his name among all nations, beginning at Jerusalem."

The word translated here as "re-mission" literally means the complete removal, or the "sending away", of our sins. And we have God's promise that he will "remember no more our sins and our iniquities!" (Hebrews 10:17)

If you have sincerely repented and confessed your sins, including any sexual immorality, then you have already been forgiven and cleansed from all unrighteous-ness. And God has promised that He will "remember no more" your past sins, so why should you have to wait until your former spouse dies before you can be ordained into ministry?

Unfortunately, there are still many churches today that refuse to ordain divorced and remarried Christians or allow them to hold offices in the church.

Their theologians try to justify their position by saying that the offices in the church are "not for everyone", and that allowing divorced and remarried Christians to have leadership positions would only cause "stumbling and division" in their church. But this "holier than thou" attitude doesn't even make any sense!

Why should a divorced and remarried person, even if he did sin in the past, cause stumbling and division in the church any more than anyone else who has sinned in the past?

Why shouldn't divorced and remarried Christians at least be given a chance to be ordained or hold offices in the church?

The traditional theologians argue that the issues of divorce and remarriage are "so complex" (they have made it that way!), and the Scriptures "so unclear" (only to them!), that they are taking the "safer" position by maintaining (what they believe are) "higher standards" for those in public ministry.

While it is true that there are "higher standards" for those in ministry, they are given to protect the church and its leaders and were never intended to exalt human beings.

The qualifications given in Paul's letters to Timothy and Titus were given only to exclude from ministry those who were *continuing in sin.* They were never intended to exclude anyone because of *past sins.*

If Christians are supposed to be excluded from ministry because of their past sins, then Paul, the very *author* of these letters, would have had to disqualify himself from all ministry!

Paul admitted, "I am the least of the apostles, that am not meet [qualified] to be called an apostle because I persecuted the church of God, but by the grace of God I am what I am!" (1 Corinthians 15:19)

Later, Paul also said, I thank Christ Jesus, our Lord, who hath enabled me, in that He counted me faithful, putting me into ministry, who was before a blasphemer, and a persecutor, and injurious." (1 Timothy 1:12-13)

Is it really maintaining "higher standards" when former murderers, adulterers, criminals, and the like are welcomed into church ministry and leadership positions, while divorced and remarried Christians who live righteous lives are forever banned?

This sounds more like "double standards" than "higher standards".

And how "safe" is their view, if they reject persons who may be called by God into full time ministry? Psalm 105 reveals that God even "reproved" kings for their sakes saying, 'touch not my prophets and do my prophets no harm!"

This doesn't sound like a very "safe" position to me!

There are many churches today that still refuse to ordain divorced and remarried Christians as long as their former spouses are still living. But then, if their former spouses should happen to die, they are immediately granted ministerial credentials.

What hypocrisy!

Is this supposed to be rational Christian theology? How can the death of a former spouse possibly make the surviving partner more qualified for church ordination and ministry?

If you are one of those who have been refused ministerial credentials or church leadership positions simply because you or your spouse were once divorced, I hope my candid, and sometimes blunt, approach has helped to set you free from the legalistic "traditions of men".

But church traditions seldom change quickly, so I cannot advise you to wait until your church or denomination revises its doctrines. If you do, you will most likely be waiting for the rest of your life.

So if you really feel strongly in your heart that God has called you into the ministry, you may have to leave and find yourself another church. It is far more important that you fulfill the calling and the ministry that God has given you.

Don't let the "traditions of men" keep you from fulfilling your calling. We all want to hear Jesus say to us one day,

"Well done, thou good and faithful servant." (Matthew 25:21)

8

New Beginnings

No matter what you have done in the past, God wants to help you start over with a new life in Christ. And your spiritual "new birth" is only the beginning of new and a supernaturally abundant life in Christ.

God is like the father of the prodigal son. (See Luke 15:11-32) He rejoices greatly whenever a wayward son or daughter returns home. No matter what you have done in the past, if there is true repentance, our heavenly Father will always forgive you and welcome you back into His presence.

The apostle Paul knew personally of the awesome grace of God when he wrote the following to the church at Ephesus:

Ephesians 2:3-7 "All of us also lived among them at one time, gratifying the cravings of our sinful nature and following its desires and thoughts. But because of His great love for us, God, who is rich in mercy, made us alive with Christ even when we were dead in transgressions - It is by grace you have been saved. And God raised us up with Christ and seated us with Him in the heavenly realms in Christ Jesus, in order that in the coming ages He might show the incomparable riches of His grace, expressed in His kindness to us in Christ Jesus. " (New International Version)

The grace of God is the undeserved favor of God. It cannot be earned (Romans 4:4) but is freely given to us through faith in the supreme sacrifice of His Son, Jesus Christ.

John 1:14-17 "The Word was made flesh and dwelt amongst us .... the only begotten of the Father, full of grace and truth... and of His fullness have all we received, and grace for grace. For the Law was given by Moses, but grace and truth came by Jesus Christ."

And not only does Jesus save us from eternal punishment and give us eternal life with Him, but He also promises to all who love and follow Him a much more abundant life even while we are still here on this earth.

Jesus said, "the thief cometh not but to steal, and to kill, and to destroy; [but] I have come that they might have life, and that they might have it more abundantly!" (John 10:10)

I remember reading about a former prostitute, who was led to the Lord through a

Christian evangelistic ministry. Later she met and married a wonderful Christian man. Her husband loved his wife so much that he would write the ministry every year just to thank them! He wanted to let them know how much he really appreciated what the Lord had done for both of them through their ministry.

That is just one example of the life changing grace of almighty God! He is able to transform a life that had once been destroyed by sin and make it into a new and a much more abundant life.

If you also feel that you have wasted your life, God is not a respecter of persons. What He has done for others, He will do for you.

REJECTION

Because of the failure of their marriages, divorced people are especially vulnerable to rejection from others. While rejection for the sake of the Gospel will yield an eternal reward, personal rejection can shatter your self-esteem and keep you from receiving the full blessings of God.

If you have ever had severe marital problems or been divorced, then you probably have already experienced at least some of the emotional pain that can result from personal rejection.

Rejection is the act of discarding someone as being completely worthless or incompetent. It is the exact opposite of praise and can be done with a look of disdain or a gesture, but it is usually expressed by the speaking or writing of negative words.

Proverbs 18:21 "Death and life is in the power of the tongue, and they that love it shall eat the fruit thereof."

Words can either build you up, or they can tear you down. If they are true and believed, they will strengthen you. But if they are false and believed, they can keep you in bondage and prevent you from receiving the full promises of God.

Whenever a circus trains an elephant to accept its captivity, they begin their training while the elephant is still very young and vulnerable. They place a big heavy chain around its leg, and no matter how hard the baby elephant struggles, it cannot break free.

Then when the elephant is older, and mentally conditioned to accept its captivity, it can easily be restrained with a thin rope and a tent stake. Even though the full-grown elephant now has the strength to break free, it cannot do this because it *believes* it cannot break free.

The same thing can happen to you. You may not be bound by heavy chains like the baby elephant, but you can be just as bound by negative words if *you believe them*. So how are you supposed to deal with negative words? The answer is simple:

You just don't believe them!

Instead of believing lies, you should study the Bible and believe the truth in God's Word that will set you free.

John 8:31-32 "If ye continue in my word, then you are my disciples indeed; and ye shall know the truth, and the truth shall set you free."

God's Word is the antidote for every negative word.

It says that your Creator loves you so much that He sacrificed his only begotten Son, just so you could be redeemed and have eternal fellowship with Him.

It says that Jesus loves you so much that He was willing to pay the price for your redemption by suffering and dying on a cruel cross. How can you feel rejected if you really believe this!

Romans 8:1 "There is, therefore, no condemnation to them who are in Christ Jesus, who walk not after the flesh, but after the Spirit."

RESTORATION

If you are unhappily married, God wants to restore the love and the joy that you once had.

If you have been legally divorced or separated, and are not free to remarry, God wants to help you restore your marriage.

If you have been legally divorced, and are free to remarry, then God wants to help you choose the right partner this time.

If you have already remarried, even though you shouldn't have, God wants to forgive you and bless your second marriage.

If you have been refused ministerial credentials just because you were once divorced, God wants to set you free from the legalistic traditions of men.

If you have been ridiculed or persecuted because of your faith, you can "rejoice and be exceedingly glad; for great is your reward in heaven." (Matthew 5:12)

If your divorce or separation was the result of your obedience to God, you can rejoice even more because you shall receive "manifold more in this present time!"

Luke 18:29-30 "Verily I say unto you, There is no man that hath left house, or parents, or brethren, or wife, or children, for the kingdom of God's sake, who shall not receive manifold more in this present time, and in the world to come, life everlasting."

There is always a "wilderness" to cross (a time of testing and trials) before you can enter into the "promised land". In order to receive the full promises of God, you must have both faith and patience.

Hebrews 6:12 "Be not slothful [lazy] but be followers of them who through faith and patience inherit the promises."

Faith is your steadfast belief that God will do what He has promised, and patience is your quiet endurance until He does.

Everyone has obstacles to overcome, and delays to endure, before they can inherit the promises of God. This is because the "wilderness" type experiences are "to humble and to test you so that in the end it might go well with you." (Deuteronomy 8:16, New International Version)

The life of Abraham is an excellent example of this. He believed the promises that God had given him, but he still had to wait patiently for a very long time until he actually received them.

Hebrews 6:15 "And so, after he [Abraham] had patiently endured, he inherited the promises."

Faith comes when God reveals His promises to you (Romans 10:17), and patience comes when you quietly wait for the fulfilment of these promises. If you are anxious or complaining, then you are really not "patiently enduring".

Even God's very special people have had to wait patiently for the fulfilment of His promises.

Joseph had to patiently endure thirteen years of slavery and imprisonment before he became the second highest ruler in Egypt.

David had to patiently wait for fifteen years after being anointed by the prophet Samuel before he actually did become King of Judah. And then he had to wait another seven years before he became King over all of Israel.

Ecclesiastes 3:1 "To everything there is a season, and a time to every purpose under heaven. "

If you are considering remarriage, you must first have faith that God will answer your prayers, and then have patience until He does. Don't be in a hurry to remarry just because you may be lonely or want security.

Take your time, and really get to know the other person before you make a new marriage commitment. Remember, your next marriage will be a commitment that must last for the rest of your life.

If you are thinking about starting a totally new career, be sure to choose something that you really enjoy doing, for that is probably what God has put on your heart, As someone once said, if you choose the career that you really like, then you will never have to "work" again!

Hebrews 12:1-2 "Let us run with patience the race that is set before us, looking to Jesus, the author and the finisher of our faith, who for the joy that was set before Him, endured the cross."

Always put God first.

No matter what you do with your life, you should always make the love of God, and obedience to his Word, your first priority. Nothing could be more important. And when you love God with all your heart, you will also do the following:

You will love God's Son.

John 14:9 "He that hath seen me [Jesus] hath seen the Father."

You will want to live right.

John 14:21 "He that hath my commandments, and keepeth them, he it is that loveth me; and he that loveth me shall be loved of my Father, and I will love him, and will manifest myself to him."

You will love your fellow man.

1 John 3:17 "If a man says, I love God, and hateth his brother, he is a liar; for he that loveth not his brother, whom he hath seen, how can he love God, whom he hath not seen?"

You will want to help people.

1 John 3:17 "But whosoever hath this world's good, and seeth his brother have need, and shutteth up his bowels of compassion from him, how dwelleth the love of God in him?"

You will become more like Jesus.

Romans 8:29 "For whom he did foreknow, he did also predestinate to become conformed to the image of his Son."

The greatest gift, other than eternal life, is to become more like Jesus. And when you live for Him and help others, you demonstrate your love for God, while at the same time, you reveal the love of God to the people you help.

Most of us do not have high profile ministries, but we all have people whom we can help.

God may already be speaking to your heart to visit a neighbor, make new friends, pray for the sick, comfort those in nursing homes, provide meals for shut-ins, help the unemployed become self-supporting, visit or write to prisoners, do or support missionary work, help support ministries that feed and clothe the poor, sing in the choir, teach

Sunday School, or maybe even join a new church.

And don't think that God has forgotten about your own personal desires. He takes great pleasure in the prosperity of His servants (Psalm 35:27), so you can expect Him to inspire you to do new things that also benefit yourself.

He may even be speaking to your heart right now to dress more attractively, take better care of your body with proper diet and exercise, take some educational courses, start a new business or career, go to college, move to a new city, take a vacation, or even do recreational things like painting, music, jogging, aerobics, tennis, golf, swimming, basketball, baseball, etc.

Above all, the Holy Spirit will always glorify our Lord Jesus Christ (John 16:14) and inspire you to tell others about His saving grace and how He has changed your life.

NEW BIRTH

If you have picked up this book just because you were interested in the subject of divorce and remarriage, but have never personally experienced the love of God and the forgiveness of sins, I want to tell you about how you can have a spiritual "new birth" and be assured of eternal life.

Jesus was referring to this "new birth" when He said to a man named Nicodemus the following statement:

"Verily, verily, I say unto thee, except a man be born again, he cannot see the kingdom of God!'"

Nicodemus did not understand what this meant, so he said, "How can a man be born when he is old? Can he enter the second time into his mother's womb and be born?

Jesus answered him, "Verily, verily, I say unto thee, except a man be born of water [a natural birth] and of the Spirit [a spiritual birth], he cannot enter into the kingdom of God. That which is born of the flesh is flesh [a natural birth], and that which is born of the Spirit, is spirit [a spiritual birth] " (John 3:3-6)

Jesus made it very clear that no one will ever see, or enter into, the kingdom of God if he or she has not been spiritually "born again". This is an extremely serious statement, and it should not be taken lightly.

There are only two kingdoms. One is the kingdom Of God, and the other is the kingdom of Satan. If you cannot enter into God's kingdom, then that means you will have to share the same fate as those who are in Satan's kingdom.

When Jesus Christ, who is the promised Jewish Messiah, returns again to Israel to rule and reign over all the earth for one thousand years, He will separate those who belong to God's kingdom from those who belong to Satan's kingdom.

To some people He will say, "Come ye blessed of my Father, inherit the kingdom prepared for you from the foundation of the world!"

To other people He will say, "Depart from me, ye cursed, into everlasting fire prepared for the devil and his angels! "(Matthew 25:31-41)

The everlasting fire of Hell was "prepared for the devil and his angels", and not for human beings. Satan had openly rebelled against his Creator, but man has sinned without full knowledge. Therefore, it is not the will of God that human beings should ever have to suffer the same fate.

2 Peter 3:9 "The Lord is ... not willing that any should perish, but that all should come to repentance."

Sin has separated us from having intimate fellowship with our pure and holy God, and the just punishment for rebellion against His righteous commandments is eternal separation from Him in a place that we call Hell.

God's perfect justice demands punishment for sin.

God's love and mercy provides us a way of escape.

The way that God has provided for us to become reconciled with Him is by being spiritually "born again".

Why do we have to be born again?

We are all physical and spiritual descendants of our first parents, Adam and Eve, and we have all inherited their sins, as well as the sins of our other ancestors.

At first Adam and Eve were without sin, so they had perfect fellowship with God in the Garden of Eden. But God had given them free will, so He tested their obedience by giving them a commandment not to eat the fruit of a certain tree in the garden. He warned them that if they did, they would surely die. However, they did not believe God so they ate the fruit thinking that they would gain more knowledge.

This was a case of direct disobedience, and the first willful sin by man against God. Their fellowship with God was then broken, and the resulting spiritual and physical death has since been passed on to all succeeding generations.

Romans 5:12 "Wherefore, as by one man [Adam] sin entered into the world, and death by sin, and so death passed upon all men, for all have sinned."

As descendants of Adam and Eve, we have inherited their sins as well as those of following generations. We were all born with the same inclination to sin as our parents and we have even added some more sins of our own.

Romans 3:10-23 "As it is written, There is none righteous, no not one... But now the righteousness of God without the law is manifested... even the righteousness which is by faith of [in] Jesus Christ unto all who believe, for there is no difference. For all have sinned and come short of the glory of God, being justified freely by His grace through the redemption that is in Christ Jesus."

Jesus is the only way to have eternal life.

John 3:16-18 "For God so loved the world, that He gave his only begotten Son, that whosoever believeth in Him should not perish, but have everlasting life. For God sent not His Son into the world to condemn the world, but that the world through Him might be saved. He that believeth on Him is not condemned; but he that believeth not is condemned already, because he hast not believed in the name of the only begotten Son of God."

The Bible says that there is only "one mediator between God and men, the man, Christ Jesus." (1 Timothy 2:5) And Jesus also made this very clear when He told his disciples, "I am the way, the truth, and the life; no man cometh unto the Father [God] except by me." (John 14:6)

No church or religion can save you. The apostle Peter confirmed this when he said, "There is no other name under heaven given among men, whereby we must be saved." (Acts 4:12)

Even good works cannot save you! The apostle Paul said, "For by grace are ye saved through faith; and that not of yourselves, it is a gift of God; not of works lest any man should boast." (Ephesians 2:9)

History has recorded that Peter and the other disciples were willing to be tortured and killed, rather than deny their faith in Jesus Christ. How could they do this if they had any doubts? And if the disciples were themselves deceivers, wouldn't at least one of them admit it in order to avoid torture and death?

BORN AGAIN

Now the question is, "What do *you* believe?" Do you believe Jesus is who He said He was? If you do, then do you want to receive Him now as your Savior and be "born again"? Although there is no set formula for being "born again", the following are four Scriptural steps to help you receive:

1. Repent (turn away from willful sins)

2 Peter 3:9 "The Lord is not slack concerning His promise, as some men call slackness; but is longsuffering to usward, not willing that any should perish, but that all should come to repentance."

2. Believe (believe that God's Son died for your sins)

Romans 5:6-9 "Christ died for the ungodly... but God commended His love toward us in that, while we were yet sinners, Christ died for us. Much more then, being justified [declared righteous] by His blood, we shall be saved from [God's] wrath through Him."

3. Receive (receive Jesus as your own personal Savior)

John 1:12-13 "But as many as received Him [Jesus Christ], to them gave He power to become children of God, even to them who believe on His name; who were born, not of blood, nor of the will of the flesh, nor of the will of man, but of God."

4. Confess (confess your faith in Jesus
    Christ to others)

Romans 10:9-13 "If thou shalt confess with thy
mouth the Lord Jesus and believe in thine heart
that God hath raised Him from the dead, thou
shalt be saved."

If you are not sure whether or not you
have really been "born again", just pray the
following prayer or a similar prayer in your
own words:

*Lord God, forgive me for my sins and cleanse
me from all of my unrighteousness. I believe
your Son Jesus Christ suffered and died on a
cruel cross to pay the penalty for my sins.*

*Jesus, come into my heart and be the Lord of
my life. With the help of your Holy Spirit, I
want to live the rest of my life doing your
perfect will.*

If your prayer was sincere, then your
sins have now been forgiven, and the Spirit of
Christ has come into your heart. (Galatians
4:6, John 14:23)

Although we are saved by grace
through faith, and not by our own works, the
Holy Spirit within you will now inspire you to
do good works and live righteously.

Ephesians 2:8-10 "For by grace are ye saved
through faith; and that not of yourselves, it is the
gift of God. Not of works, lest any man should

boast. For we are His workmanship, created in Christ Jesus unto good works, which God hath before ordained that we should walk in them."

The "religious" do good works out of *fear* to fry to gain God's favor.

We do good works out of *love* because we already have God's favor!

How do I know that I have been born again?

You will know this intuitively because the Holy Spirit will confirm to your human spirit that you are a child of God. But even if there are days when you don't feel like you have ever been "born again", you can always trust in God's Word, for "it is impossible for God to lie." (Hebrews 6:18)

The following Scriptures give assurance you have been 'born again" and have eternal life:

1 Romans 8:15-16 "For ye have not received the spirit of bondage again to fear, but ye have received the spirit of adoption, whereby we cry, Abba, Father. The Spirit himself beareth witness with our [human] spirit, that we are the children of God."

John 5:10-13 "He that believeth on the Son of God hath the witness in himself ... He that hath the Son hath life; and he that hath not the Son hath not life. These things have I written unto you that believe on the name of the Son of God, that ye may know that ye have eternal life!"

John 3:37 "All that the Father giveth me [Jesus], shall come to me; and him that cometh to me [Jesus] I will in no wise cast out!"

John 10:27-30 "My sheep hear my voice, and I [Jesus] know them, and they follow me. And I [Jesus] give unto them eternal life; and they shall never perish, neither shall any man pluck them out of my hand. My Father, who gave them to me, is greater than all, and no man is able to pluck them out of my Father's hand, for I and my Father are one!"

I will leave you with a blessing from my own heart:

May the Lord bless you and keep you.

May the Lord make his face to shine upon you, and be gracious to you.

May the Lord lift up his countenance upon you, and give you peace.

Amen.

You Can Also Read Robert Eldredge Sr.'s
book on Love& Forgiveness!

Christian Love – Christian Forgiveness

Is available at

Choicepublications.org

Breathofalmighty.org

Amazon,

Barnes & Noble

Booksellers around the globe!

www.ingramcontent.com/pod-product-compliance
Lightning Source LLC
Chambersburg PA
CBHW020233130626
46549CB00005B/1870